The American Theatre Wing
Presents

The Play That
Changed My Life

The American Theatre Wing
Presents

The Play That Changed My Life

America's Foremost Playwrights on the Plays That Influenced Them

edited by Ben Hodges

AMERICAN
THEATRE
WING
Founder of the Tony Awards®

APPLAUSE
THEATRE & CINEMA BOOKS

AN IMPRINT OF HAL LEONARD CORPORATION
NEW YORK

Published in 2009 by Applause Theatre & Cinema Books
An Imprint of Hal Leonard Corporation
7777 West Bluemound Road
Milwaukee, WI 53213

Trade Book Division Editorial Offices
19 West 21ˢᵗ Street, New York, NY 10010

The Tony Awards are a registered service mark of the American Theatre Wing, Inc.

Jonathan Larson is a registered trademark of Skeeziks, Inc.; used by permission.

Credits and permissions can be found on pages 177 to 178, which constitute an extension of this copyright page.

Printed in the United States of America

Book design by Mayapriya Long, Bookwrights
Cover design by Mark Lerner

Front cover photos, clockwise from top left: Richard Thompson as Carl, Cherry Jones as Anna, and Joe Mantello as The Third Man in the 1992 Circle Repertory Company production of Paula Vogel's *The Baltimore Waltz*. (Gerry Goodstein); Stockard Channing as Ouisa and James McDaniel as Paul in the 1990 Lincoln Center Theater production of John Guare's *Six Degrees of Separation* (Brigitte Lacombe); Jason Robards as Murray and Sandy Dennis as Sandra in the 1962 Broadway production of Herb Gardner's *A Thousand Clowns* (Shel Secunda); Diane Venora as Hamlet in the 1982 Public Theater production of *Hamlet* at the Anspacher Theatre (© Martha Swope); Everett Quinton (left) and Charles Ludlam (right) in the 1984 Ridiculous Theatrical Company production of Charles Ludlam's *The Mystery of Irma Vep* (Steve and Anita Shevett). Photos courtesy of the John Willis Theatre World/Screen World Archive.

Library of Congress Cataloging-in-Publication Data

The American Theatre Wing presents The play that changed my life : America's foremost playwrights on the plays that influenced them / edited by Ben Hodges.
     p. cm.
   ISBN 978-1-55783-740-0 (pbk.)
   1. Dramatists, American—20th century—Biography. 2. Authors, American—20th century—Books and reading. 3. Influence (Literary, artistic, etc.) 4. Playwriting. 5. Authorship. 6. Drama--Technique. 7. Drama—History and criticism. I. Hodges, Ben (Benjamin A.) II. American Theatre Wing. III. Title: The play that changed my life.
   PS129.A546 2009
   812'.5409—dc22
   [B]   2009032452
   www.applausepub.com

The Play That Changed My Life

Well that's a complex task. Probably the seventy-five masterpieces written throughout history, and the hundreds and hundreds of lesser works that have taught me what not to do. But I think I have to go back to my first theatrical experience to get to the true answer. When I was six years old, I was taken to the now nonexistent Hippodrome Theatre in New York City to see a musical called *Jumbo*. It starred Jimmy Durante and a small elephant, who resembled each other considerably, though Mr. Durante had more lines. The score, as I recall, was by Rodgers and Hart, and had lots of good stuff.

I think what hooked me—and this was long before I knew it had hooked me—was the total unreality of the experience becoming absolute reality. The absolute suspension of disbelief which took my six-year-old mind by storm.

My first Chekhov, my first Beckett, my first whatever else, were revelatory experiences. But I have to go back to Durante and this little elephant for the true genesis.

Edward Albee

Editor's Note

A note about the production photographs contained in this book: every attempt was made to find original production photographs from specific productions that are mentioned within each respective piece. In some cases, they never existed, and in others, if they did, they have been lost. In that case, photographs from noteworthy or original productions were substituted, so that at least there is, for the reader, a visual reference point. Alternately, sometimes more than one referenced production photograph was available, in which case some chapters contain more than one photograph.

CONTENTS

Foreword

by Howard Sherman

HOWARD SHERMAN, who conceived this book, has been executive director of the American Theatre Wing since 2003, where his duties have included executive producing the *Working in the Theatre* television series and cohosting the Downstage Center radio program. He has previously held management positions at the Eugene O'Neill Theatre Center, Geva Theatre, Goodspeed Musicals, Hartford Stage, Manhattan Theatre Club, and the Westport Country Playhouse.

....

I can say, without exaggeration, that I have wanted to read this book for eighteen years.

Obviously it was not sitting on my bookshelf all that time, simply waiting for the right weekend to delve into it. It existed in my mind, prompted by my dissatisfaction with another book which actually did sit on my shelf. That book had a remarkably similar title to the one you are now holding, except that it was about movies, not plays.

I do not recall precisely how I came into possession of the film book, only that I had no opportunity to peruse it before owning it. It may have been the result of a hurried foray to the basement of the Strand Bookstore in New York, a regular stop on my trips into the city from Hartford, where I was the public relations director at Hartford Stage. It may have also been a gift from a friend in PR at Random House, who kindly slipped me review copies of books on theatre and film.

Why did the movie book prove disappointing? There was nothing wrong with it, I'm sure, in the eye of literary readers: it collected pieces by essayists and short-story writers offering tales of formative years and the place that movies took in those years. But in my memory (I haven't read it many years), it was filled with too many reveries by people in whom I had no interest. Yawn. I felt cheated by the book, because I didn't care why a fiction writer or essayist liked a particular movie—I wanted to know why Martin Scorsese was moved by a certain film, or what might have led to David Cronenberg's startling visions, or prompted Steven Spielberg's benevolent view of the world.

But, more important, I wanted to know about the people in *my* business—what instilled a love of theatre in them, what sparked their passion for theatre, how did they come to be who they are? And as is true of all theatre, the work begins with the playwright, so my longed-for, as yet unwritten book would focus on authors telling us anecdotes that might contain the seedlings of why they chose to tell stories on the stage.

To my younger self, grumbling about a book that failed to fulfill my biased expectations, this would not be an impossible task. After all, *I* have long known the precise moment the theatre bug truly bit me: a rainy night, no high school homework, a friend with a car, available student rush tickets at the Yale Rep—which led me unaware into the world of Sam Shepard's *Buried Child* and out of the drama club repertoire of *The Odd Couple* and *Bye Bye Birdie*. To say that nothing prepared me for the gothic, supremely dysfunctional family drama that played out before me would be an understatement. These people had issues that far surpassed anything in my own experience, and there wasn't a therapist in sight. These folks were funny, they were scary, they were dying, both literally and spiritually—and indeed one, as the title told me, was already dead.

To this day, I can call up in my mind's eye flashes of the show. The seemingly complete, dilapidated farmhouse. The father staring into the flickering blue light of an old TV. A one-legged man chasing down another, who brandished the former's prosthetic limb. The final tableau of a hulking, childlike man carrying the ragged remains of his sacrificed, incest-born infant slowly,

Left to right: Ford Rainey as Dodge, Tony Shalhoub as Vince, and Clarence Felder as Bradley in the 1979 Yale Repertory Theatre production of Sam Shepard's Buried Child. *(Photo by Eugene Cook, courtesy of the John Willis Theatre World/Screen World Archive)*

oh so slowly, up the endless staircase as the lights faded. And, most vividly, a man, in order to terrorize and violate a young woman, inserting what in my memory was his entire hand into the mouth of this terrified girl.

This was, to borrow a phrase from, of all places, Mario Puzo's *The God-father*, my thunderbolt, when my passion for theatre burst into full being. And if it had happened to me as a teenager unprepared for the power of Sam Shepard and still lived in the aggressive press agent who worked simply to be close to theatre, surely creative artists had their own stories to tell.

So I held on to this idea, continuing to watch bookshelves at the Strand, at the Drama Book Shop, at Barnes & Noble, expecting the book I longed for to appear. I felt both expectant and apprehensive as I saw similar books about concerts, about books themselves, coming out. *The Play That Changed My Life* was always around the corner, waiting to fulfill me and disappoint me, though in this case the disappointment would be prompted not by content, but only by my own inability to have realized the book myself.

Well, life takes funny turns, and as my career took me from Hartford Stage to Goodspeed to Geva Theatre to the O'Neill Theater Center and finally to New York City and the American Theatre Wing, that same disap-pointing movie book was schlepped with me, move by move, taunting me, even after much better-enjoyed volumes were sold to cut down on space and weight. Along the way, I had the opportunity to meet countless artists who welcomed me into their world even though I was not an artist myself, but a fellow-traveler on the road of theatre nonetheless.

When I found myself at the Wing, I began to believe that it was finally time for *The Play That Changed My Life* and that I had a platform for bring-ing it into being. After all, a key element of the Wing's mission is to give voice to artists talking about their craft and their careers. Thanks to support from the Wing's steadfast and imaginative board of directors, led by chairman Ted Chapin, and from Applause Books, I have at last read the book I wanted so badly eighteen years ago.

But the most important recognition goes to the playwrights who are contained in this volume, and I thank you one and all. You are our storytell-ers, and communities gather around you to help tell your stories, as other groups gather to hear and see the stories told. I am a proud member of both of those communities. You are also but the tip of the iceberg, with countless peers also filled with stories to tell, stories both of characters and of them-selves. I hope to see and hear those, too.

My theatrical epiphany, my thunderbolt, came on the proverbial dark and stormy night. But in the theatre, a room with no windows, it is always dark until playwrights bring us into the light.

PREFACE

by Ben Hodges

BEN HODGES is editor-in-chief of *Theatre World*, the annual pictorial and statistical record of the American theatre and the recipient of a 2001 Special Tony Honor for Excellence in the Theatre. His other publications include *The Commercial Theater Institute Guide to Producing Plays and Musicals* (with Fred Vogel), *Forbidden Acts: Pioneering Gay and Lesbian Plays from the Twentieth Century* (a finalist for the 2004 LAMBDA Literary Award for Drama), and *Outplays: Pioneering Gay and Lesbian Plays from the Twentieth Century*. An actor, director, and producer, Hodges has also served as the executive producer of the Theatre World Awards for outstanding Broadway and Off-Broadway debut performances, as well as for the LAMBDA Literary Foundation "Lammy" Awards for excellence in LGBT publishing.

....

Six Degrees of Separation is not only the play that changed my life—it is also such an absurdly blatant metaphor for this project that I am tempted to make up something less on point. John Guare's magnum opus about a real-life con artist who impersonates Sidney Poitier's son in order to gain entrée into the life (and bank accounts) of the New York social elite spun me around like a top when I saw it for the first time in November 1990. Everything, including—but not limited to—race, class, and generational conflicts bombarded my senses and shook me as well as everyone else in the crowd of Upper West Siders out of the martini-induced haze through which they had stumbled into the theatre ninety minutes before. I did not know if I was more nervous for me, watching a subplot of a struggle about sexual identity while embarking on one of my own, or for the theatre full of Jackie O's with whom I was sitting and who I thought must have felt just as naked as the hustler onstage, their class being skewered right before our very eyes.

The point of the play, of course, is that we are left to wonder whether the upper echelons of New York society really differ so much—or are so far removed—from the huckster who tries to infiltrate it. (I waited on him in a restaurant once, the real-life David Hampton on whose life *Six Degrees* is based, a few years after he became a cause célèbre and before he went to jail for his crimes. He was strikingly attractive, articulate, and intelligent. And his credit card worked. I always wondered if Guare ever knew how well he got it right.) The point of the metaphor is that I would have never imagined in my wildest dreams starting out in this business that I would be lucky enough to get to know the elite group of writers I have through working on this publication—without having done something sinister to accomplish it.

I thought of *Six Degrees* many times while I worked on this project. As I sat down to formulate the wish list for this book with William Craver of the Paradigm Agency and board member of the American Theatre Wing, and Howard Sherman, executive director of the American Theatre Wing, who asked me to edit this compilation, I remembered the first question posed by my professor in my very first college theatre class: name a prominent living American playwright. At the time I could not even think of a single one. And although I have become a bit more knowledgeable about the theatre than I was at seventeen (or even before I began this project), I secretly wondered whether I could pull off the challenge of getting some of the most successful playwrights of our time to sit down and tell their stories for little reason other than that I asked them.

Like many from humble beginnings with dreams of being someone greater than they are, I had an insatiable curiosity to glimpse the intimate stories of the enigmatic writers that I had long dreamed of knowing; they were the names that Howard, William, and I bandied about as potential contributors to this publication. I hoped I would encounter scores of playwrights with stories as disparate from one another as they were from mine, but from the greatest writers of our time, and compelling, as I now know they are. I was not disappointed.

Everyone in this book partially does what they do because it is just plain fun to be somebody else for a little while, and the theatre is where people go to be somebody else. Writing for the theatre is for those who like to spin, and hear, a good yarn. These writers, from backgrounds nearly as different as can be imagined, were drawn to the theatre because the theatre is for storytellers, and these are the best in the business. They were drawn to this book because books on theatre ensure that stories will continue to be told.

This is an unprecedented publication, containing substantive essays and interviews by writers who have collectively received over forty Pulitzer Prizes,

Tony Awards, and Obie Awards. These are not snippets or afterthoughts or sound bites from press junkets that have been thrown together to sell copies of books. I wanted this book to be an opportunity for the most celebrated writers of our time to share their stories as another way for them to inspire the next generation of artists, who, in turn, will ultimately change the next generation of lives. Chances are you hold this book in your hands because you, like all of us, enjoy a good story. So it seems we are not so far removed from one another after all.

Left to right: Stockard Channing as Ouisa, James McDaniel as Paul, and John Cunningham as Flan in the 1990 Lincoln Center Theater production of John Guare's Six Degrees of Separation *at the Mitzi Newhouse Theater. (Photo by Brigitte Lacombe, courtesy of the John Willis Theatre World/Screen World Archive)*

INTRODUCTION
by Paula Vogel

For her play *How I Learned to Drive*, PAULA VOGEL received the 1998 Pulitzer Prize for Drama, the Lucille Lortel Award, a Drama Desk Award, the Outer Critics Circle Award, and the New York Drama Critics' Circle Award for Best Play, as well as her second Obie Award. It has been produced all over the world.

Vogel's other plays include *The Long Christmas Ride Home, The Mineola Twins, The Baltimore Waltz, Hot 'n Throbbing, Desdemona, And Baby Makes Seven,* and *The Oldest Profession*. In 2004–2005 she was the playwright-in-residence at the Signature Theatre Company in New York, which produced three of her works. Her new play, *A Civil War Christmas*, was produced at New Haven's Long Wharf Theatre in November 2008, directed by Tina Landau.

She is currently playwright-in-residence at the Yale Repertory Theatre, as well as an artistic associate at Long Wharf Theatre.

Theatre Communications Group has published three books of Vogel's work: *The Mammary Plays, The Baltimore Waltz and Other Plays,* and *The Long Christmas Ride Home. A Civil War Christmas* will be published in the spring of 2010.

Vogel has won numerous awards, including the 2004 Award for Literature from the American Academy of Arts and Letters, the Obie Award for Best Play in 1992, a Rhode Island Pell Award in the Arts, a Hull-Warriner Award, a PEN/Laura Pels Foundation Award, a Pew Charitable Trust Senior Award, a Guggenheim Memorial Foundation Award, an AT&T New Plays Award, a Fund for New American Plays Award, a Rockefeller Foundation Bellagio Center Fellowship, several National Endowment for the Arts Fellowships, a McKnight Fellowship, a Bunting Fellowship, and a Governor's Award for the Arts. Recent awards include the Stephen and Christine Schwarzman Legacy Award for Excellence from the Kennedy Center and the Thirtini Award from 13P. She is a fellow of the American Academy of Arts and Sciences.

Vogel is the Eugene O'Neill Professor of Playwriting (adjunct) and chair of the playwriting department at the Yale School of Drama.

⋯⋯

This book documents desire: the moment writers-to-be were caught in the tantalizing web of theatrical allure.

We are an obsessive lot, playwrights. I have stood by salmon runs, watching the leaps and twists that the fish execute, to somersault upstream against all odds, in order to spawn in the place of origin. And as I watch this marvelous feat, what do I think about? Theatre.

Of course, were I in, say, a cathedral in Rheims, I most likely would be standing in front of the stained glass thinking about *Murder in the Cathedral*.

One of my camping companions, Kathy, might helpfully remark, "You ain't right." Only the possibility of death down the rapids during my camping treks knocks the thoughts of theatre and reviews out of my head.

I suspect, reading these essays, I am not alone in my obsessive resolve. Whatever turns on the switch? How do we get so firmly imprinted on the improbable career of playwriting?

Often, desire is taught to us by our parents.

"We're gonna see shows!" Donald Margulies' parents told him, and that, he explains, "meant, of course, Broadway. (We were cultural Jews; the only fervor that existed in our household wasn't centered on religion but on show business.)"

David Auburn, whose father was a Sheridan expert, obviously saw theatre from an early age; Pete Gurney's look at his parents' relish of theatre clearly fed the flame.

But sometimes, it is seeing our parents onstage: whether performing in the church basement, as David Henry Hwang did, or in the form of a thrilling green apparition, as of Beth Henley's mother, who picked her up from school without taking time to change out of her Green Bean Man costume. For Christopher Durang, it was hearing his mother and her friends read *Hay Fever* in the living room. Seeing her mother perform as the nurse in *Romeo and Juliet* would, in fact, give Sarah Ruhl a subversive viewpoint down the road about Aristotelian protagonists: "It was strange to see my mother howl in grief . . . which perhaps gave me a displaced point of view, of who the main character might actually be in a tragedy."

We're taught desire as well by our community. "The contract that binds the audience to the work . . . is based on social ties. The play is an occasion to exercise social bonds, rather than the other way around," continues Ruhl. In David Hwang's memory, "I watched people with Asian faces working as actors in a time when such an idea was almost inconceivable in America."

Often the desire catches hold at a time when artists are seeking someplace to forge identity that mirrors their community but is absent from the

Gordana Rashovich as Emma and Rebecca Schull as Fefu in the 1978 American Place Theatre production of Fefu and Her Friends, *written and directed by Maria Irene Fornes. (Photo by Martha Holmes, courtesy of the John Willis Theatre World/Screen World Archive)*

American theatre, as articulated by Charles Fuller: "'What if we have something to say that doesn't necessarily fit into the look, feel, and sound you think English ought to have? Can we still call it English?' . . . 'Change could be brought about through the literature, "that art and specifically, writing, is the proper place to create the alternative to what is."'"

How magnified is the desire we feel when, relegated to the margins of popular culture, our identities never created onstage, we finally stumble upon a small black box that at long last feels like home? "Dear Mr. Ludlam," a younger Doug Wright pens as a note to leave with the mounds of flowers at Ludlam's Sheridan Square Theatre upon Ludlam's early death, "when I heard your characters speak for the first time, I started to find my voice, too."

Of course, we also learn as adolescents to desire the artists who act in our community theatres. Everything the Puritans feared when they attacked Elizabethan theatre is true, as evidenced by the early experience of David Auburn: "One fantastic night, an impossibly older actress—was she thirty?—perched on the arm of the chair I was sitting in and quietly took my hand in mid-conversation and slipped it up her shirt." And as stunning as the seduction might be at the cast party, the effect of seduction in actual performance is life-changing, as Diana Son attests upon seeing Diane Venora: "Seeing Hamlet as a young man but knowing, as if it were a secret, that he was being played by a woman engaged me viscerally. . . . I was being worked on alchemically."

And sometimes we are being alchemically changed by an older writer, as in this instance that a young David Ives witnesses an exchange between a woman in the audience and an American playwright: "'Mr. Albee,' she said, 'you keep using the phrase an educated taste. What do you mean . . . ?' 'What I mean by an educated taste,' Edward Albee said fluidly, 'is someone who has the same tastes that I have.' How. Cool."

For me, something started stirring when, in elementary school, I saw a telecast of Mary Martin playing Peter Pan. It reinforced my resistance to all the conventions of being a girl; the dresses my mother made me wear, the injunctions to be good, quiet, demure: I knew, having watched Ms. Martin, that girls, too, could crow. Girls could be brave. And best of all, Ms. Martin, performing Peter, a woman performing in drag, could win Wendy. Decades before our current postmodern age, Mary Martin gave me a glimpse of gender as performance.

If girls could be brave and crow, we could grow up to be playwrights. For me, it would be decades before I saw the fearlessness and performance of gender that a flying Martin revealed in green tights displayed by a playwright. I was working as an assistant to Wynn Handman, who was the artistic director of the American Place Theatre—my first job in New York. The job's one great perk was free admission to the plays (and occasional peeks at rehearsals). I didn't love the plays done that season; but Handman (and Julia Miles, who founded the Women's Project) did strange, antirealist, wild plays. And I began to hear a woman's name whispered with reverence in the halls: Maria Irene Fornes. And so one night I went into the theatre to see this new play with a strange title: *Fefu and Her Friends.*

The first act was interesting, but scarcely revolutionary: eight women, former college friends, meet in Fefu's living room to plot a theatre educational program. But then came the second act: suddenly ushers divided the audience into four parts and led us up on the stage: instead of a box set, an entire house had been constructed. And we witnessed four interactive scenes, repeated in every room of the house, until we could grasp the multifaceted relationships we had only glimpsed in the living room. There was no one protagonist; instead, Irene Fornes vivisected the same moment in time with four perspectives. Where, in act 1, I had watched a two-dimensional set, I now sat as a member of the house inside that house, which that seemed alive and intimate.

More than that, Fornes had created one of the characters as a young working-class lesbian with the name of Paula. I had the eerie sensation that someone I had not met knew me well, knew of the still-recent sting of rejection I'd suffered as a working-class woman struggling at Bryn Mawr College (Fornes' Paula graduated from that Seven Sisters' academy; I had not). When the character Paula vented in an outburst against her well-heeled classmates' sense of entitlement, I found myself weeping in my seat.

I could feel every assumption I had about what made a play being shattered. I left the theatre realizing that plays could be written that were not cognitively understood, but emotionally felt. In the years to come, I never did understand a play that Irene Fornes wrote. But I felt them, intuited them, responded to them through my body.

It is outside the purview of this book; but *Fefu* and Fornes did more than change my life. The real question that has driven me, and many of us in the field, is: After the first rush of theatrical addiction, how do we sustain a life in the theatre? Over the decades, I have had glimpses of Irene, on panels, in the theatre, in person, doing the impossible: as a woman who loves women, she constructed a body of work, directing her plays, finding the space and the money, teaching, and mentoring; and without excuses, despite never being underwritten by the commerce of theatre, year after year, she wrote the next play and the next.

There are two people who have kept me in the field: Peter Franklin, who was my agent for the past twenty-five years, who recently has left the business of agenting, but not, as those of us who know and love him, the avocation of mentoring and caring for American playwrights. And then there is Irene Fornes: her example, her body of work, her keeping on, which helps to sustain me to face the blank page. At a time when women playwrights still face odds as improbable as salmon swimming upstream, Irene Fornes has blazed a fierce, passionate path to follow.

1
......

DAVID AUBURN

Photo by © Joan Marcus

DAVID AUBURN's plays include *Proof* (2001 Pulitzer Prize, Tony Award, and New York Drama Critics' Circle Award), *An Upset* (2008 Ensemble Studio Theatre Marathon), *The Journals of Mihail Sebastian*, and *Skyscraper*. Films include *The Girl in the Park* (writer/director) and *The Lake House*. His short plays have been collected in the volume *Fifth Planet and Other Plays* (Dramatists Play Service). His work has been published in *Harper's, New England Review*, and *Guilt and Pleasure*, and he was a contributing editor to *The Oxford American Writer's Thesaurus*. A former Guggenheim Fellow, he lives in New York City.

Little Rock

I was seventeen. We were living in Little Rock, Arkansas, and I set our VCR to record a PBS broadcast of a play I had read about in the TV listings. It sounded odd and interesting and I had never heard of it: *The House of Blue Leaves*. A play from the early '70s, evidently, but a new production on Broadway. I couldn't watch the broadcast live because I was working late at the theatre.

I was already deeply involved in the theatre, albeit with absolutely no interest in pursuing it professionally. I just liked hanging around actors and working backstage. I had even found ways to earn a little money doing it.

We had moved to Little Rock the year before. It was my family's second move in two years. If you move a lot you look for ways to make friends quickly, to plug yourself into familiar social situations. Sports do this, but I wasn't much interested in sports. Theatre was better. My brother and I figured this out—try out for the school play, or go down to the community theatre and ask to help out. It was something to do. The adults in charge were often eccentric and entertaining. You stayed up late, got a buzz from the performance energy even if you weren't performing. You got to climb ladders wearing tool belts. Girls were involved.

And Little Rock was a good theatre town. It had two professional theatres. One, the Arkansas Rep, didn't hire teenage stagehands, but I found work there a couple of times a year working their benefit dinners as a busboy. (One night I walked into the dining room with a bag of ice on my shoulder for the bar and got a nod from the governor, Bill Clinton.) If you worked the dinner you could go to the show. At the Rep I saw productions of modern plays like *Quartermaine's Terms* and *The Night of the Iguana*.

These plays were interesting but, like the much older plays I had been taken to growing up and was more familiar with (my Dad was an English professor and his academic specialty was Sheridan, so I'd seen four or five productions of *The School for Scandal*, a bunch of Restoration plays, and lots of Shakespeare), the experience of seeing and enjoying them never shook me from my vague and strangely firm conviction that my future career path lay in international diplomacy.

I'm not sure how I formed this notion of my future career, or even what the notion was, exactly—myself as some sort of high-level envoy or international aid worker, maybe. That I spent no time at all working in or even reading about this area, and spent a great deal of time hanging out at theatres and acting in school plays, didn't remotely impose on my assumption that theatre was a hobby that I'd abandon as soon as I went to college and got serious about my international relations studies.

The second of Little Rock's professional houses was the Arkansas Arts Center Children's Theatre, and I spent much more time here. It had a permanent repertory company of six or seven actors, and a group of maybe fifteen or twenty teenagers hung around to perform in the shows or work backstage. If you worked on a show at the AAC you got permission to skip school to run the matinees. Being a children's theatre, all the performances were matinees. That meant ten or twenty days of driving downtown to the theatre instead of to high school. You felt like a professional, going to work.

The Children's Theatre didn't pay, but when the Arkansas Opera Theatre took over the Arts Center's auditorium for their three or four annual productions, they needed experienced sound- and light-board operators. They didn't care that I was seventeen. I worked *Rigoletto*, *The Barber of Seville*, *A Little Night Music*. I was hired—miraculously, *paid*—to run the Arts Center's primitive boards. These boards drove the lighting designers brought in from New York or Chicago insane. They were used to writing hundreds of

Clockwise from top: Julie Hagerty as Corrinna, Stockard Channing as Bunny, John Mahoney as Artie, and Swoosie Kurtz as Bananas in the 1986 Lincoln Center Theater production of John Guare's The House of Blue Leaves *at the Vivian Beaumont Theater. (Photo by Brigitte Lacombe, courtesy of the John Willis Theatre World/Screen World Archive)*

cascading computerized cues. In Little Rock they were limited by the speed at which a teenage board-op on his knees in front of a manual preset bank could enter the individual dimmer settings—up to twenty per preset, and up to twenty presets. It was nerve-racking to be yelled at by these anxious, aggressive pros demanding that you keep the fuck up, but exhilarating to find that you could.

More important even than the practical experience, if you hung around the professionals enough you got invited to their parties. Here were adults who talked to us seriously about life and art; and more to the point gave us wine and cigarettes and let us make out on their couches, and sometimes flirted with us themselves. One fantastic night, an impossibly older actress—was she thirty?—perched on the arm of the chair I was sitting in and quietly took my hand mid-conversation and slipped it up her shirt.

So why, given the fact of all this highly stimulating immersion—of my de facto high-school-age semi-professionalism—did I remain oblivious to the possibilities of a career in the theatre? Why did it take a VHS recording of a Broadway revival shown on TV to tip me toward something approaching the beginnings of professional ambition?

I still have the tape I made of the broadcast. Watching it again now, and rereading the play, it is clear *The House of Blue Leaves* is about ambition—about fame, and the hunger for recognition and success. But this is not what struck me at the time. It barely registered.

What registered—and it was with real shock, when I finally watched the tape, late at night after getting home from a show—was the play's sheer, overwhelming exuberance. I had never seen a "serious" play with such an utter lack of solemnity or restraint. It was nothing, *nothing* like the thoughtful, well-tailored contemporary classics that I saw at the Rep. It seemed *crazy*, inexplicable—a farce with songs, direct address to the audience, a kid who wanted to blow up the pope, a deaf movie star, a chorus of angry nuns, a character called Bananas.

Nor could I figure out how to reconcile the play's overflowing high spirits with the despair at its core, or the shocking, violent ending. *The House of Blue Leaves* is a despairing play. All the characters are grievously afflicted by illness and terror, beset by humiliations and frustrated longings of the most agonizing kind. How was it that this darkness coexisted alongside such loony hilarity—and not merely coexisted, because it wasn't just that the terror and the jokes didn't conflict with one another, they actively generated one another—the jokes becoming expressive of the terror and vice versa?

After many viewings, I decided, provisionally, that maybe the simplest way to explain the play was as a demonstration of the utility of jokes. Jokes could do anything, or everything—illuminate character, provide exposition, generate plot, establish a logic that went beyond conventional explanations of motive and allowed the playwright to go places he wouldn't otherwise be able to go.

Here is Bananas' act 1 explanation of how her "troubles all began":

> I drove into Manhattan . . . Forty-second Street. Broadway. Four corners. Four people. One on each corner. All waving for taxis. Cardinal Spellman. Jackie Kennedy. Bob Hope. President Johnson. All carrying suitcases. Taxi! Taxi! I stop in the middle of the street—the middle of Broadway—and I get out of my [car] and yell, "Get in. I'm a gypsy. A gypsy cab. Get in. I'll take you where you want to go. Don't you all know each other? Get in! Get in!"

It goes on from there. There's a laugh on nearly every beat. It's like a succession of punch lines, but cumulatively the surrealism of this near-stand-up monologue becomes a better explanation of Bananas' frustrated longings than any realistic explication could. (And in Swoosie Kurtz's performance in the production I saw, the jokes were almost unbearably painful.) A string of jokes; but, John Guare seemed to be saying: see what jokes can do?

I liked this explanation because it fit with another intense interest I had. My father, the Sheridan scholar, was also crazy about comedy. Comedy LPs were the other entertainment staple of my childhood, the soundtrack, to my mother's occasional annoyance, of every family car trip—Monty Python, *Beyond the Fringe*, Bill Cosby, Tom Lehrer, Richard Pryor, Steve Martin, and (my favorite) the manic and possibly actually insane Jonathan Winters. My brother and I memorized the bits and made best-of cassettes and entertained or irritated our friends with our own renditions.

Much later, I read Guare's own explanation of the origin of his play: seeing, on successive nights, the Royal National Theatre of Great Britain's productions of *Dance of Death* and *A Flea in Her Ear*, and wondering, "Why shouldn't Strindberg and Fedyeau get married, at least live together, and *The House of Blue Leaves* be their child?"

Maybe an analogous fusion eventually occurred for me, triggered by seeing *The House of Blue Leaves*—of those endlessly spinning comedy records with their endless jokes, and the experiences in those Little Rock theatres where I spent so much time. Why shouldn't they belong together? Why shouldn't the source of so much fun also be the place where you go to work?

The next year when I got to college in Chicago I was bored to tears by my International Relations course. I looked for a theatre. There was a student sketch-comedy group on campus. I auditioned and got in. I started trying to write my own scenes, my own jokes.

One of my first weeks in town, I noticed *The House of Blue Leaves* was playing in Evanston. It was hard to get to. I took the bus downtown, then the El, then another bus. Getting there took an hour and a half. The production was disappointing. I didn't care. I was out in the city and going to plays. On the long train ride home I could think about the scenes and jokes I would try to write for my troupe. Maybe eventually the scenes would get longer and my jokes better—better meaning not just funnier, but capable of doing more than one thing at a time. Maybe I'd try to write a play some day.

2

JON ROBIN BAITZ

Photo by Jon Robin Baitz

JON ROBIN BAITZ's plays include *Mizlansky/Zilinsky*, *The Film Society*, *The Substance of Fire*, *Three Hotels*, *The End of The Day*, *A Fair Country*, *Ten Unknowns*, and *The Paris Letter*. Baitz is a Guggenheim Fellow, a Pulitzer Prize finalist, and an American Academy of Arts & Letters award winner. He has received a Humanitas Prize for the PBS production of *Three Hotels*, which he directed. After writing episodes of *The West Wing* and *Alias*, Baitz created the award-winning ABC drama *Brothers & Sisters*. He also wrote the screenplays for the film adaptation of *The Substance of Fire*, as well as the Al Pacino drama *People I Know*. He is the distinguished visiting artist at the New School's graduate drama division, where he also teaches television writing.

On Reading and Seeing Plays

I first became interested in plays by reading them, not by seeing them. Though I do remember being so moved at a production of *Pinocchio* at age five that I could not restrain myself from leaping up from my seat and bellowing a white lie, "Don't you eat that boy, my daddy is a cop!" at two poor actors co-joined in a large and lumpy papier-mâché-and-cloth gray whale. Said whale was clumsily poised to swallow the overly florid and somewhat girlish and flouncy puppet. In retrospect, Pinocchio was most likely a real live actress.

In high school, in the highly unlikely locale of Durban, South Africa, I saw, at age sixteen, in a tiny theatre in the City Hall, a strange and overwrought production of *Kennedy's Children* by Robert Patrick. The homosexual "themes," viewed right next to my parents, caused me to run away from the theatre and from sex for at least a week, and in the case of the latter, a year. I would have no part of it. Acting in *The Man Who Came to Dinner*, in a cloud of white hair powder and perched in a wheelchair from which I mugged like Al Jolson, further compelled me to look at plays and players as a mug's game, not fit for Prince Robbie. Later, at the virtually professional theatre department at Beverly Hills High School, I essayed my Preacher/Judge in a production of Lanford Wilson's *The Rimers of Eldritch*, which, when I read it alone under a tree, seemed urgent and mysterious and foggy, but which onstage, played by the thespians of 90210, did not measure up. In eleventh grade, the Hamlet in my head was perfection; a handsomer, fitter version of me, with my moody hair and an aristocratic hauteur and a Bowie/Lou Reed/Belmondo cool. Better than Olivier in tights *any day*. Or so I thought. So was Konstantin, (again, my avatar), dying slowly over seagulls, the general absence in his life of art, conversation, recognition, or even love.

Maybe, who knows, I was just hard-wired for turning the glyphs in a script into a kind of music. A small gift. On the page you know what the pause is filled by. You know what lives in the silence. You recognize the temperature of menace and of lust and of love and passions otherwise easily mucked up by goddamn actors in overheated makeup. Probably I had not acclimatized to performance yet, and the unsettling intimacy of great acting. I had a gimlet eye, and a cool one, critical and closed. On the page it's totally clear what the playwright's parenthetical asides are really about. You know how the interruptions and negotiations and secrets combine to set the mood, and just how the clothes hang, what that black chair placed just so means, the way the cigarette smoke catches the light on stage, and more than anything, you can arrange the whole thing perfectly. When you read a play, you see, you are, if not its God, at least, its demigod.

I suppose I had begun absorbing Saul Bellow's dictate that "a writer is simply a reader moved to emulation." If Mamet's *Glengarry Glen Ross* was in New York, and I was poor and in L.A., it didn't matter at all; the Grove edition was as precious to me as a pre-glasnost samizdat journal to a hungry Kiev poet, alive with a hugely enticing staccato and bravery, vulgar male energies, vivid with desperate American dreams being dashed on the sharp rocks of market forces and denuded machismo, the two Achilles' heels of the American century. And I do think *Glengarry Glen Ross* surely set me loose to listen *very carefully* to the stumble-down, shtick-laden patois of the two down-and-out producers I worked for in Beverly Hills, and on whom I based my first play, *Mizlansky/Zilinsky*. Mamet just taught me how to be a kind of lock picker, a thief of the *actual*. It was David Hare who won my heart. The day I read *Plenty*, I was left shaken by the seemingly limitless theatrical possibilities it presented. I finished the play, quietly awed by the weird joy of recognition that this young playwright (he was thirty-one when it opened in London, I was twenty-three when I read it) had found a singular path through the gooey earnestness and empty hectoring which have, more often than not, made politics on stage embarrassing to behold. It was also the very first time I wished I could have *seen* the production, which had run at The Public and then on Broadway the following season, where, despite having been championed by Frank Rich, it ran for eleven previews and ninety-two performances, all the proof I needed that Broadway was no longer the venue of choice for contemporary drama. Here was a playwright whose moral outrage was upholstered in sophisticated enough fabric; as tense as the play makes you, with Susan's "psychiatric cabaret," it is nevertheless very funny. *Plenty* is structured cleanly, with twelve scenes, all of which are reduced to their emotional and physical essentials. They are stripped of ornamentation, and devoid of artifice. *Plenty* dispenses with the turgid convention of worrying about linear time. The scenes, about the end of an empire and the ideals of a nation, move in time as dizzyingly as Susan's own sanity. The plot is easy, and virtually devoid of exposition: A seventeen-year-old Englishwoman, a courier for the French Resistance, is dropped behind German lines in 1943. And following that, no other moment in her life has real meaning. She cannot have children. She is bored by the meaningless of the work she undertakes in bombed-out, recovering London, and she marries a kind and patient diplomat, whom she proceeds to punish as though he were Britannia herself. Even lunatics need an audience, not to mention a warm body to lie against at night. Again, for reasons too painful to explore here, I understood the vertiginous pull that the mental illness of a loved one can have on those around them. Through it all, Hare strips away the hypocrisies and seemingly inexhaustible empty formality of his postwar Britain through Susan's Hedda-like hegira toward madness. Perhaps it was— again—recognition; I got it. I had lived in colonial Durban for most of the '70s, gone to school where there was corporal punishment, uniforms, and a kind of indolent hostility to the reality on the ground there. Perhaps my Durban was a satellite for the particular and bitingly brittle Englishness Hare describes perfectly. In a note to the published version the play, Hare writes that "irony is central to the English humor, and as a people we are cruel to each other, but always quietly." Each scene somehow hinges on that cruelty, that endgame. And David's rage is so beautifully modulated throughout that what one experiences is not the bludgeoning whiskey-sodden grimness a prior generation of English playwrights traded in, the "Angry Young Man" Osbornian fury, or the exquisite blunt ellipses of Pinter, but rather, for me, a precision, grace, and originality of the author's "testimony." Hare's writing was rigorous, his people singularly articulate, and the combined effect was,

*Kate Nelligan as Susan Traherne and Edward Herrmann as Raymond Brock in the
1983 Broadway production of David Hare's* Plenty. *(Photo by Martha Swope, courtesy
of the John Willis Theatre World/Screen World Archive)*

to me, magically theatrical. I found myself having to shake off his rhythms and shed the youthful anxiety over my own developing voice which led me to mimic his. A shameful admission, but there it is. A young writer, if he is not careful, can become merely a reader moved to self-immolation *through* emulation. *N'est pas*, Mr. Bellow? It seemed to me at the time to be a breakthrough play for the author. I could just feel it somehow. He had made the leap into a kind of writer's maturity. Years later, in David's *Skylight*, which also broke my heart, a mellower sadness presided, one in which love, plenty, romanticism, and idealism still cannot be meshed with the hardest of truths, but here there is a kindness that seems equally earned and equally wise. In retrospect, twenty-five years on after reading *Plenty*, I suppose David's modus vivendi somehow lit a path, maybe it's projection on my part and the natural urge a young writer has to find heroes, but I was somewhat emboldened to explore America through our mercantile culture, our systems, and how they fail.

Kate Nelligan, who starred in *Plenty*, did a TV play of mine, *Three Hotels*, for American Public Television and arranged an introduction with David when I was in London. His first words to me, a sly smile on his face, were, "So, it seems we share Kate Nelligan, don't we?" I laughed. That, I thought, was the least of it.

I do not mean this as afterthought, but Wally Shawn's *Aunt Dan & Lemon*, read around the same time, further got under my skin. I say this laughing, but I thought, "Fuck it, if this man can write these long hallucinatory monologues, well, I can too." Wally also was spectacularly conflicted by the conventions of our easy lives, our unlived lives, our imaginary deals with ourselves, in a way I got. Maybe it's because we were both aware of how lucky we were to be born white and male and American, and also slightly disgusted by the passport that entitled us too. One day, I was walking down Seventeenth Street, carrying in my book bag his play *The Fever*, and we slightly knew each other, and I was absurdly excited to pull it out and make him sign it. He laughed, his brilliant cartoon features coming alive, and it was like a moment from a cartoon in *The New Yorker* in his dad's day, when two guys meet on the street, and the one guy signs his play for the younger playwright, with a bravura flourish, "To Robbie on the day of the INCREDIBLE coincidence."

The fact of it is I love playwrights and we are really brothers and sisters. It's so absurdly hard. And so absurdly out of sync with the rest of the larger meaner world, in the neatest way. I love the graduate students I work with at the New School, and how they're trying to carve out something brand new, out of the dislocation and overstimulation of being young now, I love it when

I see Neil Simon and he tells stories of productions past, and I feel lucky to have had a few meals and drinks with Arthur Miller and to have listened to him bitch about audiences, and I love that Suzan-Lori Parks and Tony Kushner and Chris Durang and Rich Greenberg and I can smile at each other in a particular way, when we run into each other. Like we get the joke, and it's a really fucking long one.

3

......

NILO CRUZ

NILO CRUZ is a Cuban American playwright whose work has been produced widely around the United States and Europe. His plays are many and include *Night Train to Bolina*, *Dancing on Her Knees*, *A Park in Our House*, *Two Sisters and a Piano*, *A Bicycle Country*, *Hortensia and the Museum of Dreams*, *Lorca in a Green Dress*, *Anna in the Tropics*, *Beauty of the Father*, *A Very Old Man with Enormous Wings*, and translations of Lorca's *Dona Rosita the Spinster*, *The House of Bernarda Alba*, and *Life Is a Dream*. He is currently writing the book for the musical *Havana*, with music by Frank Wildhorn, and a screenplay about Alina, daughter of Fidel Castro. Nilo has been the recipient of numerous awards and fellowships, including two NEA/TCG Theatre Residency Program grants, a Rockefeller Foundation grant, San Francisco's W. Alton Jones Award, and a Kennedy Center Fund for New American Plays Award. His work has been seen at the McCarter Theatre in New Jersey, New York Shakespeare Festival's Public Theater, Manhattan Theatre Club, and Repertorio Español, as well as South Coast Rep, Arena Stage in Washington, D.C., Alliance Theatre in Atlanta, New York Theatre Workshop, Magic Theatre, Minneapolis Children's Theatre, Oregon Shakespeare Festival, Washington's Studio Theatre, and Florida Stage. Internationally, his plays have been produced in London at the Hampstead Theatre, the Finborough Theatre, the Royal Academy of Dramatic Art, and in cities throughout Spain, including Madrid and Seville. In 2003 he won the Pulitzer Prize for Drama for his play *Anna in the Tropics*, and in 2009 he won the PEN/Laura Pels Foundation Mid-Career Award.

Distilled to Its Essence

Ben Hodges: I am interested in going back a little to the beginning of what your dramatic influences were, in your early childhood in Cuba, and before you came to America, if there were any, or did it start after you got here that you became interested in the dramatic arts?

Nilo Cruz: I don't recall seeing any theatre in Cuba. I do remember being exposed to the world of entertainment. When I was a child—I was eight or nine years old—my family always went to the beach in the summer; it was a ritual, and my father used to rent a family room at a famous hotel called Hotel Internacional in Varadero Beach. I was ten years younger than my sisters. They were already engaged around that time, and in the evenings my whole family loved going to the hotel's cabaret to dance and enjoy the show, including my grandmother. This meant that nobody wanted to stay home and babysit me. So one evening my father said, "We'll take him with us tonight. We'll take him to the cabaret. I have friends there. We'll sneak him through the kitchen and it's going to be all right." And they did. They sneaked me through the kitchen and basically hid me under the cabaret table, where my family was sitting, which was covered in a white tablecloth. Then, when the lights went off in the cabaret, and the show started, I lifted the tablecloth and started watching the show. The waiter of course saw me, smiled and said, "It's okay. Let him stay. Let him watch the show." And that was the first time I saw live entertainment. I was just amazed to see all the lights, to see the showgirls, and it wasn't just the kind of dancing that you see in Las Vegas—the dancers danced ballet too. I was just dazzled by the vibrant music, by the exuberant energy coming from the stage.

Hodges: It must have seemed rather magical for a kid.

Cruz: More than magical. It was astounding. Intoxicating. Imagine being a little boy and being exposed to this energizing and powerful music, and all the colorful images coming from the stage, including lots of flesh from the showgirls. So when I went back home, I gathered some friends from the neighborhood and I put on a show on my grandmother's patio. Basically that was sort of the seed, my first attempts to recreate what I had experienced and witnessed on a stage. Actually, now I am writing a libretto for a musical that is set in a nightclub in the 1950s, *Havana*, and I constantly travel back in time to those early impressions—the lushness of that first cabaret show I ever saw.

Hodges: And I am wondering if you had exposure to—did you have a television?

Cruz: Yes, we had a TV.

Hodges: But this must have been very different from anything you had seen on television, or was it different because you were there?

Cruz: This was very different because there is nothing like live entertainment. It is ritualistic. It is in your face, basically, and it was just so powerful to see that bigger-than-life energy pouring out of the stage. And the magic of the mirrored ball, before they became popular in discos. [*Laughs.*] It was so spectacular. I was also exposed to concerts because my sister's fiancée was a musician, and I got to go to the theatre several times to hear him play the piano. I am from the province of Matanzas, and the municipal theatre there is gorgeous. It's a magnificent neoclassical building, built in the mid-1800s.

Hodges: Were you exposed to plays at school?

Cruz: No. I wasn't exposed to any plays at school—not until much later, when I came to the States. The circus, yes. I got to see the Russian circus, which was very exciting.

Hodges: Was there a lot of reading going on in your household or at school that may have influenced you?

Cruz: Not so much in Cuba, but when I came to the States I became fascinated by literature and by books, and I actually volunteered to work in the library to be close to books in my sixth grade. That's when I discovered a poem by Emily Dickinson, and I thought to myself, this what I want to do; I want to write poems.

Hodges: And you came to America when you were ten?

Cruz: I was nine, about to turn ten.

Hodges: And how did your writing life develop from there? What were you first experiences when you got here, when you were in Miami?

Cruz: I was writing poetry before I started writing plays. I was working at a hospital, and in between patients I would jot down ideas or write a verse. Then one day I had an epiphany that I had to go to the theatre. That night I went to the regional theatre in Miami at that time, which was the Coconut Grove Playhouse, and I saw *The Dresser*. As a result of that experience, the next day I decided to enroll at a drama school at Miami Dade College. There I met a wonderful teacher who guided me in the right direction. Instead of doing scenes in class from Tennessee Williams or Chekhov, I would write my own scenes. And my professor said to me, "You really ought to study playwriting or directing." Because I was also directing my own work. This professor was the one who also gave me my first opportunity as a director, and I directed a couple of plays by Hispanic playwrights at this college.

Hodges: And when did your work with Maria Irene Fornes start?

Cruz: It started in Florida. I had two drama teachers—the professor who told me that I should go into playwriting, and then I had another professor who had a professional theatre, and she asked me to direct a piece for her company. The piece was *Mud*, by Maria Irene Fornes. In conjunction with the college we were able to bring Maria Irene Fornes to do a workshop at the school. When I took the workshop with Irene, I gather she noticed my potential as a writer, so she asked me to join her writing workshop at INTAR in New York. But she said the workshop would start on Monday, and I had met her on Friday. [*Laughs.*] At this time I had changed jobs, and I was working at a cargo airline . . . believe me, not the most interesting job. And of course, I couldn't resist the opportunity of studying with Fornes. Immediately I called my boss and I said, "Listen, I have got a great opportunity to go to New York and study with a playwright that I admire." And he said, "Well, you know what is best for you." So I borrowed a winter coat from a friend—I didn't even have a heavy coat, because you don't need one in Florida. [*Laughs.*] I bought a plane ticket. I called a friend here in New York and asked her if I could crash on her living room couch. I got here to New York on Sunday and then started the workshop on Monday at INTAR with Fornes. I studied with her for three years. And as a result, my life changed.

Hodges: And what's really interesting to me here is that you seemed to just start playwriting almost immediately upon learning about the art, whereas someone else may not have done that for years, if ever, and I am wondering what gave you that kind of confidence, if that is what it was?

Cruz: I believe I had a second epiphany, when I was directing Irene's play in Florida. I just adored the economy and the rhythms of the language. I loved how cinematic *Mud* is, and the theatricality of the piece. It's a short play, but very powerful. I knew after directing *Mud* that I wanted to be a playwright.

Hodges: Am I right that at the point when you moved to New York, you hadn't seen many productions by contemporary playwrights?

Cruz: Actually, in Miami, I was exposed to a lot of Iberian writers through the Hispanic Theatre Festival. For instance, the Spanish writer Fernando Arrabal was a favorite. Emilio Carballido from Mexico was another playwright I adored. Then there were other experimental companies from Chile, Argentina, Spain, that brought excellent and fascinating theatre to south Florida. The

Patricia Dolen Gross and Juan Cejas in the 1987 SEAT (South End Alternative The-atre) production of Maria Irene Fornes' Mud in Miami, Florida. (Photo by Nilo Cruz)

theatre from Latin America and Spain is more lyrical and expressionistic; it is less grounded in the kind of realism that we are familiar with in this country.

Hodges: When you started with Irene, did you feel like there were many more things you needed to learn before you could continue as a playwright?

Cruz: It is necessary for writers to find a routine, to find different ways of entering the writing process. In other words, you can't depend on the muse to come to you. As writers we have to search and find inspiration every day. Irene provided the lab members with a series of exercises that would invoke the initial inspiration. What is wonderful about studying with her is that her approach to playwriting is not so much about rules, or formulas. It's not about, "This is the way to sculpt a play," or "This is the traditional three-act form." Her focus as an instructor was very much about opening the imagination and allowing us to run with the imagination, then eventually for us to encounter the play through the process of writing. The actual sculpting of the play was done when we had a series of scenes. It's really a lovely approach.

Hodges: So there wasn't some sort of artificial structure imposed.

Cruz: No. Thank God.

Hodges: It sounds like a really wonderful thing.

Cruz: Absolutely, and the process was not intimidating like what you were talking about. We weren't trying to emulate any particular structure or writer.

Hodges: How long was it, after you were in New York, before you found yourself at Brown University?

Cruz: I studied with Irene for three years. And then Paula Vogel, who was the head of the playwriting program at Brown University, asked Irene if she had any participants in the lab that were interested in going back to school. I wanted to continue studying, so I applied to the master's program at Brown and was accepted.

Hodges: In New York, were you seeing a lot of theatre other then the work you were doing at INTAR? Was there anything that jumped out at you in a good way?

Cruz: I saw *Uncle Vanya*, done by the State Theatre of Lithuania, at the Joyce Theater. I just adored that production. It was delicate and yet so powerful. It was elegant, and playful, the way that Chekhov should be "sadly playful." That is one piece of theatre that really stands out for me. And I also saw a lot of work at LaMaMa. The Greek plays that were directed by Ellen Stewart—I thought those were wonderful.

Hodges: I am wondering if there is something about this training element of Irene's work, or the feeling you were given of the newness of not only the culture of New York City, but maybe what was going on with you personally, that made it more possible for you to explore your work at that particular time?

Cruz: *Mud* is not a play that I would identify with, because it takes place in rural America. It has nothing to do with my sensibility as a person or as a theatre practitioner. But there is something behind the craft of this piece which really struck me. The structure is quite cinematic, and yet it is very theatrical. It's actually pure theatre, because it has been distilled to its essence. As a director I was fascinated by the rhythms of the language, the visceral and cruel life it presents. And even though the play takes place in rural America, there is something about the sensibility of *Mud* that feels like it comes from my country. And Irene is Cuban. There is something about the generosity of spirit, the attention to specific details that speaks to me, especially when the character, Mae, says that she wants to die in a hospital with injections. Very simple lines, but the dignity behind those lines, I understood very well, which is basically the dignity that I have identified with Cuban people.

Hodges: Pride.

Cruz: Pride, yes. All of Irene's plays have been a source of inspiration. Irene has been a guiding light for me. She has been a role model. The fact that she came to this country at an early age and was able to cross over as a playwright was something for me to look up to. As an artisan in the theatre, I wanted to move away from the Hispanic plays that I was directing in south Florida. I wanted to speak to a larger audience, and I felt that the only way to do that was to write plays in English. And this is what Irene was doing not only as a playwright, but as an educator at the INTAR lab. She was nurturing Latino playwrights. It was the perfect environment for me.

4

......

CHRISTOPHER DURANG

CHRISTOPHER DURANG has had plays on and Off-Broadway, including *A History of the American Film* (Tony nomination), *Sister Mary Ignatius Explains It All For You* (Obie Award), *Beyond Therapy, Baby with the Bathwater, The Marriage of Bette and Boo* (Obie Award, Dramatists Guild Hull-Warriner Award), *Laughing Wild, Durang/ Durang* (evening of one-acts), *Betty's Summer Vacation* (Obie Award), *Mrs. Bob Cratchit's Wild Christmas Binge, Miss Witherspoon* (2005 Pulitzer finalist), and *Adrift in Macao* (book/ lyrics Durang, music by Peter Melnick). His latest play, *Why Torture is Wrong, and the People Who Love Them*, premiered at The Public Theater in 2009. In recent years Durang has won the Harvard Arts Medal and the Dramatists Guild Fund Madge Evans/Sidney Kingsley Playwriting Award, and he was the 2008 honoree at the William Inge Theatre Festival. Durang has acted in movies (*The Butcher's Wife, Housesitter, Mr. North,* and *The Secret of My Success*) and in his own plays. He appeared with Sigourney Weaver in their coauthored *Das Lusitania Songspiel* (Drama Desk Award nominations for both of them), and with Julie Andrews in the Stephen Sondheim revue *Putting It Together* at Manhattan Theatre Club. He acted in the premieres of *The Marriage of Bette and Boo* (Ensemble Acting Obie Award) and *Laughing Wild* (opposite E. Katherine Kerr, Jean Smart, and Debra Monk). With John Augustine and Sherry Anderson, he performed his crackpot cabaret *Chris Durang and Dawne* multiple times, winning all three of them a 1996 Bistro Award. With Marsha Norman, he has been cochair of the playwriting program at the Juilliard School since 1994. They jointly won the 2004 Margo Jones Award for their work with emerging playwrights. He is a member of the Dramatists Guild Council. His Web site is www.christopherdurang.com.

The Incipient Existentialist and the Broadway Musical

I can't say there was a play that "changed my life" . . . but I do think my life was changed by my early love of theatre.

And so I want to write about two Broadway musicals I saw and loved when I was thirteen years old in 1962, the satiric and delightfully manic *How to Succeed in Business Without Really Trying* and the sweet and somewhat dark *Carnival!*

First, though, I should explain I loved theatre before seeing these shows because my mother loved theatre, and musicals in particular. When she was a young woman she saw the original *Oklahoma!* on Broadway, and she just adored that.

And she read plays too—she thought Noël Coward was hilarious (as well as sophisticated), and she actually invited friends over to our house to read his play *Hay Fever* out loud. It remains my favorite Coward play to this day, and my first memory of it was hearing Helen Levinson, the lively and rebellious editor of the local newspaper, read the leading part of the self-dramatizing actress Judith Bliss in our living room. Helen was about seven feet tall, had attractive Arlene Dahl-red hair, and a slight Texas accent; but she also had flair and humor, and the Coward lines really came out of her mouth most amusingly.

I'm pretty sure my mother read the supporting role of Jackie, the friendly but dizzy young woman invited to the house by David Bliss, the husband of Judith. The entire Bliss family has invited houseguests of the opposite sex for the weekend, in order to flirt openly in front of one another—though the family eventually loses interest, and the unhappy guests end the play by sneaking out, stung and horrified by their not-so-blissful treatment. So grand gestures, bon mots, and rudeness—a very satisfying mix for a play.

My mother, born in 1922, had a crush on the 1920s and wished she had been a young woman then, and a flapper. Her favorite musical was *The Boy Friend*, and I listened to her recording of the Julie Andrews Broadway version. And we eventually saw a revival Off-Broadway at the Cherry Lane which my mother and I found delightful, especially whoever played Dulcie—another dizzy part, rather like Jackie.

My mother's favorite comedienne was Gracie Allen, and she greatly enjoyed these muddle-headed characters. In moments when life was going well, she enjoyed being dizzy and free-associative around people, though she also had a side that was strong and smart and confrontational; and I find I'm constantly drawing on her personality when I write women characters.

Anyway, my mother's love of theatre imprinted itself on me. When I was seven or eight, I was taken to the Paper Mill Playhouse in Millburn, New Jersey, near where we lived. That theatre—still thriving in 2009—had good professional productions, and I saw a version of *Oklahoma!* there, as well as *The King and I, Damn Yankees, Peter Pan,* many others. And we were about an hour from New York City and Broadway, so a few times a year, I was taken to see Broadway musicals, sometimes with both my mother and father. And sometimes just with my mother.

The first Broadway musical I saw was *Fiorello!* with music by Jerry Bock and lyrics by Sheldon Harnick. I adored the song "I Love a Cop" for some reason—it was sung by a subsidiary character, but I loved the melody and the joyful exuberance of the song as performed by Pat Stanley.

There was also the lovely song "'Til Tomorrow" (easily hummed after one hearing), and an even prettier, somewhat contemplative song called "When Did I Fall in Love?," sung movingly by Ellen Hanley as LaGuardia's wife, who realized she fell in love with her husband only after they'd been married—her love crept up on her. Her character sadly dies—minutes after this realization, in my memory. (Minutes after in terms of the storytelling, I mean. I don't mean she sang the song, and dropped to the floor. Though I might write something like that.)

And then the last song about romance came from Patricia Wilson as the ever-present, ever-ignored secretary Marie, who has pined after her boss, LaGuardia, for the entire show. And right before she finally gets her man, she has a great "to hell with it all" song in which she vows to marry "The Very Next Man." For some reason, I was always stirred by these ladies in musical comedy who were carrying unrequited torches for their leading men—like Miss Adelaide waiting 107 years before finally marrying Nathan Detroit in *Guys and Dolls.*

Anyway, will I ever get to talking about *How to Succeed* and *Carnival!* All right. I will. Soon. But first . . .

I started writing plays at age eight. The first one was two pages; and my Catholic parochial school put it on one afternoon; that sounds rather Montessori of them, doesn't it? By age eleven, my plays tended to be twenty to twenty-five pages, and a bit more complicated. And seeing movies and seeing musicals had become a major pleasure in my life. And sometime in 1962 I was taken to a matinee of *How to Succeed.*

How to Succeed in Business Without Really Trying won the Pulitzer Prize for Drama the year it opened—most unusual for a musical—and its funny book was by Abe Burrows, Jack Weinstock, and Willie Gilbert; and the music and lyrics were by Frank Loesser. It's not his most melodic score, actually, but it's a very good match for Burrows' shiny, stylized book, which follows J.

Pierrepont Finch, who rises from the mail room to head of the company by manipulating everyone around him.

Part of the musical's success came from the inspired casting of Robert Morse in the lead role. Morse's look was cute, not handsome, and with a devilish glint in his eye. He also had one of those singing voices just right for the role—it wasn't pretty or impressive, but he hit the notes right, he had great comic intentions behind the way he sang the lyrics, and he sounded like a real person, not a Good Singer.

Of course, for some roles, a "Good Singer" can be great—Mandy Patinkin, for instance, was glorious singing the beautiful songs in Stephen Sondheim and James Lapine's *Sunday in the Park with George*—another musical that won the Pulitzer Prize.

But Morse was just what *How to Succeed* needed.

And as a thirteen-year-old, I just adored him, and found him so funny yet also endearing. You just rooted for him as an actor; and the tone of the musical, though sharp, was not angry—we knew this was an exaggeration of how big business worked—and so his goofy charm was just right for the show. It was benignly amusing that all these businessmen were foolish, were selling something inexplicable called "wickets," and were mostly focused on their coffee breaks and their attractive secretaries.

(Big business didn't seem as insanely destructive back in 1962 as it appears to have become in our more recent past. If we were to have a musical about the financial industry of 2007–2009, I think it would need to be in the style of *Sweeney Todd*, full of fury and murder. The friendly, amused tone of *How to Succeed* would not be the right response to our recent toxic financial meltdown.)

And as with my strange-for-a-boy empathy for the love problems of the unrequited secretary Marie in *Fiorello!*, I was very interested in the struggles of pretty Rosemary in *How to Succeed*. She didn't have the same desperation as Marie in *Fiorello!* It was just that Finch-Morse was too ambitious to pay much attention to romance. And so Rosemary had a fun "declaration of love" song called "Happy to Keep His Dinner Warm," in which she happily envisions herself as a semi-ignored housewife, always reheating his dinner, unable to time anything because his ambitions keep him constantly late and at the office.

But as in any good musical, the melody and held notes still gave a good "I'm gonna marry this guy someday" punch to it. I saw the show with the original Rosemary of Bonnie Scott, and I remember her fondly; but the role was taken over by Michele Lee, who was successful in it and did the role in the movie, and went on to a deservedly full career.

Robert Morse as Finch (center), with members of the company of the 1961 Broadway musical production of How to Succeed in Business Without Really Trying. *(Photo courtesy of the John Willis Theatre World/Screen World Archive)*

The show got a lot of critical and comic mileage from the casting of 1930s film actor Rudy Vallee in the role of the head of the company. Vallee had a good, 1930s-reedy tenor voice, and he was a good target for Morse to focus in on—pretending to be from the same alma mater as Vallee (cue the funny song "Grand Old Ivy"); and then there was also the side plot of Vallee's extramarital flirtation, pursuing the office sexpot, Hedy LaRue.

By the time of her entrance, we had already had the funny "A Secretary Is Not a Toy" song—with early Bob Fosse funny/quirky dance moves—and now Hedy LaRue shows up as a new employee with no secretarial skills of any kind but with big bosoms and red hair, and all the men stop in their tracks when they see her. (She was a bit like Helen Levinson but without the smarts.) Eventually she does something that ruins the company—I forget what exactly, but it has to do with her knowing where the "hidden treasure" was in some publicity stunt for the World Wide Wicket Company.

Though that then leads to Finch somehow becoming head of the company, and though he could get Vallee and everyone else fired, this is a musical, of course, and so instead he embraces universal forgiveness of anyone who had anything to do with the near ruination of the company because we are all part of the—cue song—"Brotherhood of Man." This is a very rousing number with a great countermelody part for the boss' secretary, memorably sung in the original by Ruth Kobart, and even more memorably sung by the great Lillias White in the fun Matthew Broderick revival in 1995, directed by Des McAnuff.

I wrote two musicals in my high school years, with my composer schoolmate Kevin Farrell—*Banned in Boston*, written when he and I were thirteen, and *Businessman's Holiday*, written when we were fifteen or sixteen. And our Catholic school Delbarton put both on, and we put on local versions in the summer as well. And the second one—about a loyal secretary with an unrequited crush on her boss—I now see was very influenced by *How to Succeed*. Though in my version the unrequited secretary realizes her boss is a fool, and she quits her job and leaves it and him at the same time at the end of the musical. This was an unconscious reference to *A Doll's House,* since I hadn't read that yet.

But both musicals were written in a playful, semi-cartoonish style that I picked up at least partially from seeing *How to Succeed* when I was thirteen.

Now as to *Carnival!* Well, *Carnival!* spoke to my sensitive side, which I do have but only occasionally write from. (Though more so now that I'm older and weepier. My father used to cry during "Danny Boy," and I have his genes.)

Where *How to Succeed* was shiny, funny and brittle, *Carnival!* was sweet, touching, and included not just an orphan girl facing a new and scary life, but a bitter man who has shut down and only opens up emotionally after a great deal of effort, finally letting himself be changed by his feelings for this young woman. It ends up being a transformative musical, and it is one of my favorite shows.

And instead of identifying with the unrequited secretary, as I had in the earlier two musicals, this time, in what was probably a healthy development, I identified with the bitter leading man, Paul, played by the great Jerry Orbach in his youth.

The musical is directly based on the popular Leslie Caron movie *Lili* (1953), which in turn was based on a short story (and later novella) by Paul Gallico. The very good book to the musical is by Michael Stewart and is based primarily on the Helen Deutsch screenplay, which sweetened the Gallico version. (The Gallico novella, reading about it, got very dark.) The excellent music and lyrics were by Bob Merrill.

The musical book is set in France. Lili (played by Anna Maria Alberghetti) is a recently orphaned young girl, whose dying father has told her to seek out a friend who works in a traveling carnival selling concessions.

At the beginning of the show Lili discovers this family friend has just died, and the man who has taken over concessions initially looks like he'll give her a job—triggering Lili to sing the tuneful and optimistic "A Very Nice Man" song. But the Very Nice Man starts to push his attentions on her, and she is rescued by Marco the Magnificent (the dancer-actor James Mitchell), the suave, popular-with-the-ladies magician, with whom the naive Lili falls instantly in love. (She is nothing if not vulnerable and open.)

The other characters, whom we soon meet, are Rosalie, the mistress (shocking!) of Marco, and played by Kaye Ballard in what I recall as a superb comic turn. And likable Jacquot, played by Pierre Olaf (a "genuine" Frenchman, who had made a splash on Broadway with *La Plume de Ma Tante*). And then there's Jerry Orbach's role of Paul, who was injured in the war and had to give up his dreams of being a dancer; he's become dark and bitter and unfriendly, and he has reluctantly become a puppeteer. (As happens with so many bitter people.)

Lili hates Paul on sight, but when the puppets speak to her—voiced, of course, by Paul, hidden behind the puppet-theatre curtain—she is enchanted and enters a playful and hopeful world with them. (This puppet part of the story was inspired by the popular '50s television show *Kukla, Fran and Ollie*, in which a charming Fran Allison improvised weekly with puppets; her seemingly genuine rapport with the fictional puppets was the inspiration behind all the versions of this story.)

If *How to Succeed* was giddy and fun, and if *Fiorello!* was complicated but full of warm and "normal" human relationships, *Carnival!* dealt with bitterness, contemplated suicide, and the dangers vulnerability faces in the world.

Surprisingly, for a show known as "sweet," act 1 ends with Lili climbing a tall ladder to the trapeze platform, planning to jump and end her life. Lili, in the confusing thrall of her crush on Marco, has become his onstage assistant, and in her first try at it she ruins the entire grand finale and is fired by the head of the carnival. And she goes from the excitement of her first performance in the carnival to despair and once again not having a home.

I remember sitting way back in the theatre and seeing Lili climb up and up and up to the top of the trapeze platform. It was very high, and it was a spare, desolate stage picture. Lili appears to be alone onstage until suddenly the puppet Carrot Top pokes his head out of the puppet theatre and calls out her name: "Lili!" I don't recall the exact dialogue, but he encourages her to come down from the ladder and talk to him. Carrot Top is the friendliest of the puppets, and as Lili begins to be taken into this fantasy world talking to him, the other puppets come in and chat with her too—Horrible Henry the Walrus, Renardo the Fox, and Margueritte, the conceited and pretentious opera singer. In terms of distracting a suicidal person, it works.

Bitter Paul, of course, is who is really speaking, comforting, and distracting Lili. And at the very end of the act, Marco shows up to convince Lili to try to get her magician's assistant job back, but Paul's own voice—harsh and dominating—suddenly replaces Carrot Top's voice, and he tells Marco that from now on Lili will work with the puppets. While the song "I've Got to Find a Reason" plays underneath as the act 1 curtain falls.

Ah, "I've Got to Find a Reason" is Paul's first song in act 1. And as an impressionable thirteen-year-old, I was very haunted by it and its lyric:

> I've got to find a reason,
> For living on this earth.
> I've got to find a reason,
> For taking the space I take,
> Breathing the air I breathe . . .

Wow, that's a very different character introduction song from, say, "Oh, What a Beautiful Mornin'" or "A Cockeyed Optimist."

The incipient existentialist in me identified with both Paul's bitterness and his introspection. He knew he was troubled about life, and though he couldn't talk to anyone else about it, he talked to himself.

Although I hummed a lot of the songs from the show—I was and am a "hummer" as I walk down the street—it was the lyric and melody to "I've Got to Find a Reason" that became my unconscious first choice to hum and sing. Speaking of melody, I think Bob Merrill's score to *Carnival!* is incredibly satisfying, with many wonderful melodies. He's best known as the lyricist of *Funny Girl*. And I'm sorry to say I don't know the other shows for which he wrote music as well as lyrics, which include *New Girl in Town* and *Take Me Along*.

But in this one, he writes some great songs. The song "Mira," in which Lili describes the small town she grew up in, is very beautiful and includes these poignant memories from a girl who now has no one in the world:

> I come from a town, the kind of town
> Where you live in a house 'til the house falls down
> But if it stands up, you stay there
> It's funny but that's their way there

And later:

A room that's strange is never cozy
A place that's strange is never sweet
I want to have a chair that knows me
And walk a street that knows my feet
I'm very far from Mira now
And there's no turning back . . .

In the movie *Lili*, though it was not a musical, Leslie Caron and the puppets sang the very pretty "Hi-Lili, Hi-Lo," which became a hit. Merrill had the task of writing a similar song—of sad but hopeful love—and he did a great job of doing that with "Love Makes the World Go Round" ("Somebody soon will love you, if no one loves you now"), which also became a hit.

I loved the dark songs that Paul sings. The "Her Face" song was dramatic and moving, as Paul fought himself about his feelings for Lili. In act 2, Paul is tortured by Lili's continuing interest in the untroubled, superficial Marco. Stung by hearing Lili is going to return to being Marco's assistant, Paul rehearses a new song with the puppets and Lili and is mean and cruel and makes her cry. Then suddenly kisses her. (Ah, how one hates these people who send mixed messages, no?) Lili is horrified by the slap-then-kiss and sings the aptly named song "I Hate Him," which turns out to be written to work in yearning counterpoint to Paul's beautiful "Her Face" song.

Paul's final song, after he has clearly lost her, is the mournful "She's My Love," where the lyrics show him finally acknowledging, when it's too late—and once again, only to himself—how much he loves her.

Just as the puppets save Lili from committing suicide at the end of act 1, the puppets save the ruined relationship between Lili and Paul at the end of the show. Lili has grown up and seen through the friendly but womanizing Marco, and has packed her battered suitcase, ready to leave for who knows where. She passes by the puppet theatre, and Carrot Top one more time stops her and asks why she is leaving without saying goodbye. Carrot Top confesses how much he loves her, and so do the other puppets. Lily feels the hand holding the puppets is trembling, and she pulls back the curtain to reveal Paul.

Paul, of course, is all of the puppets, and the more grown-up Lili more fully realizes this. Paul admits in his own voice that he's Carrot Top, who loves her; he's Margueritte, who's vain and jealous; he's Renardo, who's sly and lies; he's clumsy Horrible Henry, who just wants to be loved. Angry Paul can't help doing one more make-me-fail gesture, and after he expresses his vulnerability to Lili, he then hurls Carrot Top to the ground and starts to leave. Lili picks up Carrot Top and reaches her hand out to Paul. He stops and, after a moment, he reaches his hand back toward her. Orchestra swells, lights dim, curtain. I cried.

Anna Maria Alberghetti had a lovely and easy soprano, and she was lovely and easy in her acting as well as Lili, and won a Tony for her performance (sharing it in a tie with Diahann Carroll for her role in *No Strings*.)

(Wikipedia.com says Anna Maria appeared on *The Ed Sullivan Show* more than fifty different times; I feel like I saw about forty-seven of those times. Ed S. sure did repeat his favorite guests a lot. Still, it was great the way he would feature performers from then-current Broadway shows, singing numbers from those shows. With only a few TV channels we really did have a more unified popular culture then. Ah, the '50s.)

I found Jerry Orbach's performance as Paul riveting. In his youth, he was almost conventionally handsome, but with just enough cragginess to seem unusual, deeper than just handsome. He had a strong, good baritone, but it didn't sound trained, it just sounded like a regular human being expressing himself.

For those who only know him from his admirable later years as Detective Lennie Briscoe on *Law & Order*, it may be a surprise to know how frequently Orbach distinguished himself in musicals. He was the original El Gallo in *The Fantasticks* (thus on the record singing "Try to Remember" for the first time). After *Carnival!* he played Sky Masterson (the romantic role, not the Nathan Detroit one) in a revival of *Guys and Dolls* (opposite talented Anita Gillette, who stood by for Anna Maria in *Carnival!*). Then he played the Jack Lemmon role in *The Apartment* when Burt Bachrach, Hal David, and Neil Simon turned that movie into *Promises, Promises*; Orbach won the Tony for Best Actor in a Musical that year.

He was also the sleazy lawyer Billy Flynn in the original 1975 *Chicago* (nominated for a Tony) and the old hand director in the 1980 *42nd Street*. (By the way, *42nd Street* was directed by the talented Gower Champion— who also directed *Carnival!*)

Nineteen seventy-five was my first year living in New York City (after my Yale School of Drama days), and how I saw *Chicago* is one of my favorite memories of the theatrical pleasures of living in that city. I was living on West Eighty-seventh Street, subletting from Mrs. Burl Ives. (I found it in the *Village Voice*; really.) And at 7:15 p.m. I thought, maybe I can go see a musical tonight. I hopped on the subway at 7:30 and got to the 46th Street Theatre in time to buy a $10.00 "obstructed view" seat to see *Chicago*. In those days "obstructed view" meant you sat in one of those side boxes, and because you were way on the side, there was indeed a small part of the stage you couldn't see. However, the boxes were really, really close to the stage, so you could

Jerry Orbach as Horrible Henry the Walrus and Anna Maria Alberghetti as Lili in the 1961 Broadway production of Carnival! *at the Imperial Theatre. (Photo courtesy of the John Willis Theatre World/Screen World Archive)*

see the actors' faces and bodies really close up. It was very exciting. And that night I was just swept away with the brilliance and charisma of Gwen Verdon, Chita Rivera, and Jerry Orbach in that Kander-Ebb classic. Ten dollars and getting in on sudden impulse.

There's one other performer who really impressed me in *Carnival!* and it was Kaye Ballard. Marco's "mistress" Rosalie is a great part, and she has a lot of good comic zingers to speak. Ms. Ballard at her best is one of the larger-than-life comediennes, a bit like Martha Raye—like Raye, she has a gift for broad comic reactions and also a strong, killer Broadway voice. While the sensitive part of my nature was being drawn in by Ms. Alberghetti and Mr. Orbach, the part of me that loved comedy was delighted with Kaye Ballard. And we had seats way in the back, and Ms. Ballard is the sort who can Merman-style whack it to the back of the house. I thought she was just great.

And I loved when Bob Merrill took a tongue-in-cheek, easygoing love song called "Always, Always You"—sung by Rosalie and her unfaithful magician lover, while she was seated in a box and he was shoving swords through the box—and had her sing it a few minutes later alone onstage at a much slower tempo; and suddenly the same song became a full-throated torch song with actual feeling. It was Rosalie's only serious moment, and Kaye Ballard was terrific singing it.

So, dear reader, I'm sorry I've gone on and on, and been rather associative too. But I have to say that while writing this, I recaptured much of the love I felt for seeing those two musicals early in my life.

5

HORTON FOOTE

Photo by David Spagnolo

HORTON FOOTE had his first play, *Texas Town*, produced Off-Broadway in 1941. Since then he has had plays produced on Broadway, Off-Broadway, Off-Off-Broadway, and at many regional theaters. Plays include *Dividing The Estate* (Tony nomination, Obie Award, Outer Critics Circle Award), *The Last of the Thorntons*, *Young Man From Atlanta*, *The Chase*, *The Traveling Lady*, *The Trip to Bountiful*, *Night Seasons*, *Tomorrow*, *The Habitation of Dragons*, *The Orphan's Home Cycle*, *Roots in a Parched Ground*, *Convicts*, *Lily Dale*, *The Widow Claire*, *Courtship*, *Laura Dennis*, *Vernon Early*, *The Roads to Home*, *The Carpetbagger's Children*, and *The Day Emily Married*. He received Academy Awards for his screenplay adaptation of *To Kill a Mockingbird* and his original screenplay *Tender Mercies*. He received the Pulitzer Prize for *The Young Man From Atlanta*, the Lucille Lortel Award for Outstanding Achievement Off-Broadway, and the Outer Critics Circle Special Achievement Award for the Signature Series of his plays. In 1996 he was elected to the Theatre Hall of Fame. In 1998 he was elected to membership in the American Academy of Arts and Letters, and at the same time he received from the academy the Gold Medal in Drama for the entire body of his work. In 2000 he received the PEN/Laura Pels Foundation Award for Drama and the New York State Governor's Arts Award, and in December of that year he was given the National Medal of Arts Award by President Clinton. In 2006 *The Trip to Bountiful* won the Lucille Lortel Award for Outstanding Revival, and he was given the Drama Desk Lifetime Achievement Award for his body of work. His memoirs, *Farewell* and *Beginnings*, are published by Scribner's. He passed away in early 2009.

Pasadena and Beyond

The Pasadena Playhouse, at 39 South El Molino, was just half a block off Colorado Boulevard, Pasadena's main thoroughfare. The building was two-storied, of Neo-Spanish architecture, with a large patio, which we crossed to get to the theater proper. A side wing on the patio floor had shops and a restaurant; above this wing, reached by open stairs, was a small second theater called the Recital Hall. The larger theater was called the Main Stage. Also, in the building were a vast wardrobe department and a shop for building scenery. There were two houses near the Playhouse that had been turned into classrooms for theater students. It meant nothing to me at the time, but the school advertised the practicality of its training, saying, "Training is not confined to theory. Students learn by doing! Assistant direction, costuming, stage managing, scene designing, even the actual construction of painting and settings, and the work of stage crews." Advertising in national magazines, the school listed former students who had gone off to be in movies against the background of a palm tree, klieg lights, starts, a section of the patio, and the theater building itself.

In 1933, the Main Stage had been operating for nine years but the theater had been in Pasadena for seventeen years. This unique institution was an outgrowth of the enthusiasm for amateur theater that swept across America in the 1920s. Many of these amateur or "little" theaters built handsome homes themselves and had large subscription audiences. Their desperate earnestness was satirized in a popular George Kelly play of the time, *The Torchbearers*.

The Pasadena Playhouse called itself a community theater, but by the time I arrived, it was that in name only. Occasionally, it did use nonprofessional or semiprofessional actors, but most often brought in professional actors from Los Angeles or Hollywood. Gilmor Brown was the artistic director of the theater. He had been an actor in some minor stock companies around the West and, seeing the vitality of the "little theater" movement, had come to Pasadena to start one. The Pasadena Playhouse had the Main Stage, the Recital Hall (used by the senior students), the Play Box (as far as I know, the first theater-in-the-round in America), and the Padua Playhouse (run in a nearby town by students who returned for post graduate work). During my time there, I saw many interesting productions on the main stage of the Playhouse. I saw Synge's *The Playboy of the Western World*, Sidney Howard's *Alien Corn*, and Molière's *Le Bourgeois Gentilhomme*. I saw an adaptation of *The Brothers Karamazov* and several adaptations of Dickens' novels. I saw Victor Jory in Lynn Riggs' *Road Side* and Lee J. Cobb, then a very young actor, in Oscar Wilde's *Salome* directed by Benjamin Zemach of the Habimah Theatre. I also saw Walter Hampden, then our leading Shakespearean actor, in a play by Martin Flavin. He played a zookeeper in blackface. Additionally, there were many Shakespeare productions. In fact, by my second year the Pasadena Playhouse claimed to have produced more Shakespeare (thirty-two productions) than any other theater in the world except for Stratford-upon-Avon.

Our classes started at nine in the morning and continued until five. We had classes in fencing, eurhythmics, diction, costume design, makeup, theater literature, styles of acting, and scene design. We also had play rehearsals. Once a week, Gilmor Brown met with us, mostly giving inspirational talks about what a rewarding life the theater could be if one had the proper dedication. For our first play productions, we were divided into two groups. One group was assigned the play *Shakuntula,* a classic East Indian drama. My group was assigned a Roman comedy. The directors were two of the five staff directors at the Playhouse. At that time, I had read very few plays and was completely unfamiliar with Roman comedies. The rest of the students were just as ignorant of the material of the period as I was. Our director was bored with the play and with us. Not knowing how in the world to approach the material and afraid to admit that he didn't understand a word of it, he put us on our feet the first day and watched wearily as we stumbled about the stage. To make matters worse, I discovered I had a Southern accent that was difficult to understand. The rehearsals lasted six weeks and then, without props, scenery, or costumes, we presented our play on the main stage for our fellow students.

Classes were not a happy time for me, either. I had no talent for drawing, so I got nowhere with costume and stage design. Diction class was torture. All I heard was that to be an actor, any kind of actor, I had to get rid of my accent. However, the one class I enjoyed from the start was the theater literature class. Our teacher was passionate about plays as literature and very knowledgeable about Greek, Roman, Elizabethan, Noh, Chinese theater, and the theater of Molière. During class breaks, I would go to him and we would talk about literature of all sorts—plays, novels, poetry, essays, and short stories.

One day in mid-November, my speech teacher told me that she felt I need special help. She said she knew a wonderful private coach named Blanche Townsend who agreed to coach me for an hour each week. To pay for my lessons I went without lunch. In our first lesson, she assigned Browning's "Last Duchess." Although I did not agree with her methods of teaching, it was at least a system. She had her rules, and she was able to explain them. She based everything on phonetics before learning them. She was a great fan of George Bernard Shaw and, of course, thought *Pygmalion* a masterpiece. She was encouraging, and at that stage in my life, encouragement was something I badly needed.

There was a young man in one of my classes, John Forsht, from Lock Haven, Pennsylvania. He had been to college for two years and had done quite a bit of college acting. He wasn't interested in movies. He wanted to go on the New York stage; his ambition was to play Hamlet. He told me of all the great Hamlets he had heard about: Alexander Moissi, Edwin Booth, John Barrymore, and Henry Irving. I began to study *Hamlet* too, and I started to memorize the soliloquies. I asked Miss Townsend for help. She would only hear me do "Speak the speech, I pray you . . ." and I had to say "trippingly on the tongue" over and over until it almost ruined Shakespeare for me forever. Soon we had two camps in our class: those who wanted to be New York actors and those who wanted to be in pictures. We were all sure, as we argued amongst ourselves, that we would get what we wanted. Few of us ever did.

My Grandmother Brooks came to California to visit two of her sisters. She thought the boarding house I was living in was unsuitable, so she took rooms for us in Orange Grove, a very expensive part of the city. There was a lovely garden behind the house, and I used to go out there after dinner and practice my diction exercises. One night a man from next door called out in the dark, "Are you ill?" "No sir," I said. "I'm just practicing my diction exercises." "Well," he said, "Cut that out. This is a respectable neighborhood."

That winter, Eva Le Gallienne announced that she was bringing three Ibsen plays to the Biltmore Theater Los Angeles. John Forsht and my knowledgeable professional theater friends were all excited abut the event. I had never heard of her or the Civic Repertory she has founded in New York City, but I pretended that I had, and I listened to all they had to say about her.

I asked my grandmother if she would take me for my birthday. We took the Interurban into Los Angeles for the Saturday matinee performance of *Hedda Gabler*. They set the play in the late twenties, and I will never forget Le Gallienne's entrance, her hair bobbed, wearing a short skirt, and smoking a cigarette. I thought she was extraordinary in the part, and the play made a very deep and lasting impression on me. My grandmother sensed this I am sure, and she asked if I would like to see the evening performance of *The Master Builder*. I did, of course, and that night I saw my second Ibsen play with Le Gallienne again in the lead. Though I have seen many plays and many fine productions since, none have made the kind of impression on me that these first Ibsen plays did.

Eva Le Gallienne was thirty-three at this time. She had been a star in Broadway in her early twenties and she was said to be exquisite in the two Molnar plays, *Liliom* and *The Swan*. She could have continued in the commercial theater but she felt an actress could only reach her potential by playing parts in great plays, classic and modern, and in repertory. Still in her twenties, she found backers and bought a run-down theater on 14th Street in New York City. She gathered a company of actors around her and for a number of years she performed Chekhov, Ibsen, Shakespeare, and modern

European classics. She acted, directed, and produced. Her productions of *Alice in Wonderland* and *Peter Pan* were legendary. She worked tirelessly and unselfishly, and though it was difficult and expensive to keep so many actors and technicians employed, she was able to find patrons to make up all deficits, until the Depression. Then she lost her backers and patrons, and she was forced to close her theater just before she began her California tour. My grandmother bought her book *At 33* for me. In this book, Le Gallienne tells the story about the founding and running of her company. At the close of the book, I felt she was determined to start her theater again one day. She did try two more times, once in New York and once on the road. Both times, she failed, or really, I think the theater failed her. She continued acting, directing, and producing, always preaching the gospel of a repertory theater that produced serious and important plays.

The New York Theater (1930–1940)

That fall I went to New York to look for work as an actor. I had little experience: two years at the Pasadena Playhouse and a summer at the Rice Playhouse. However, there was and is one constant understanding among the theater people: Never dwell on the obstacles. And so I began to learn lessons about a part of theater the Pasadena Playhouse had not prepared me for: how to survive in an economically depressed city where the phenomenon of talking pictures, having decimated both vaudeville and winter stock companies, was now beginning to make inroads on Broadway itself. There were losses, losses everywhere.

The first thing I did when I got to New York was to make a pilgrimage to Le Gallienne's Civic Repertory Theatre in 14th Street. When I got there, I found it occupied by a left-wing theater group called "Theater Union." The Theater Union, I was to soon learn, claimed to be part of "the new theater movement." How often have I heard through the years: "This is the new theater?" This also is a truism about theater; suddenly there appears from nowhere a new concept, a new approach to acting, to directing, to producing.

It all meant little to me at the time. I wanted to be a part of the "old theater," the theater of Belasco, Frohman, Sam Harris, Winthrop Ames, and Arthur Hopkins. I wanted to be an acclaimed actor-manager, have a New York season, and then tour the country; or I wanted to be idealistic like Miss Le Gallienne and be part of a repertory company. It seemed to my young mind that the "old theater" was invincible.

In those days, the theater district ran from 38th Street as far up as 59th Street. In this district, there were lovely theaters in abundance; the Empire, the Playhouse, the Cort, the Maxine Elliott, the Music Box, the Morosco, the Belasco, the Hudson, the Henry Miller, the Booth, the Shubert, the Martin Beck, the National, the Forrest, the Ambassador, the Bijou, the Little Theater, the Forty-sixth Street Theater, the Golden. The list went on and on. Every season they were all filled with productions, not all of them successes, but few New York theaters in those days remained dark for very long. Each fall, the producers such as Sam Harris, Arthur Hopkins, Guthrie McClintic, Jed Harris, John Golden, Crosby Gaige, Max Gordon, Gilbert Miller, Brock Pemberton, and the Theater Guild announced their new productions and usually fulfilled their promises.

These days, the second balcony of a theater is rarely filled, but when I first came to New York, they were often filled. The tickets for the second balcony were fifty-five cents, and we soon learned we could look down into the orchestra for empty seats during the first part of the show, and then during intermission we would move down to the orchestra and take the vacant seat. I saw a great many plays starting from the balcony, usually ending up in the orchestra. I saw Judith Anderson and Helen Menken in *The Old Maid*; Lillian Hellman's *The Children's Hour*; John Gielgud, Lillian Gish, and Judith Anderson in *Hamlet*; and Maxwell Anderson's *Winterset*, *High Tor*, and *The Three Sisters* with Katharine Cornell, Clifford Odets' *Paradise Lost* and *Awake and Sing*, Tallulah Bankhead in *The Little Foxes*, and Ethel Barrymore in *The Corn is Green*. I also saw Sean O'Casey's *Juno and the Paycock*, in a lovely production by Dublin's Abbey Theatre, with Barry Fitzgerald and Sara Allgood, and a brilliant performance by Nazimova in Ibsen's *Ghosts*.

The New York theater had its stars then. The stars often acted in plays tailored to their particular talents. Sometimes, not often, these stars were in interesting plays. The Lunts did *The Seagull* (translated by Stark Young) and Katharine Cornell did *Romeo and Juliet*, Shaw's *Candida* and *The Doctor's Dilemma*, and Chekhov's *The Three Sisters*. All of this impressed me at the time; but as I look back now I realize that the plays were mostly superficial comedies or melodramas with a firm eye on the box office. Then I saw Laurette Taylor in a revival of *Outward Bound*. Suddenly, I began to realize that talent was abundant but genius and originality were quite rare.

It was during this time that the playwrights Maxwell Anderson, Robert Sherwood, Sidney Howard, Elmer Rice, and S. N. Behrman formed the Playwrights Company, which was to produce their plays exactly as they wanted them, or at least as they thought they wanted them. The other popular writers—Moss Hart, George Kaufman, Edna Ferber, Howard Lindsay, Russell Crouse, and Rachel Crothers—mostly formed permanent attachments to producers who cared little about what the playwright wanted from the production.

The New York theater of this era was genteel, a kind of gentleman's club, sure of itself and what its public wanted. America was in the midst of a Depression, but you would never have known it from the plays. If playwrights attempted any social commentary, it was on the most superficial level. One exception to this happened down at the 14th Street Theater where Clifford Odets' one-act play *Waiting for Lefty* was being produced. It was about a strike; and at the end of the play, the actors called on the audience to strike. The audience responded by yelling back, "Strike!" Broadway pretended it did not hear that call at all. It kept right on pouring tea in its drawing rooms.

One day in New York City I met Rosamond Pinchot, whom I had known in California. She was well known for her appearance in Max Reinhardt's *The Miracle*. She told me she was now studying at Tamara Daykarhanova's School for the Stage. She needed a scene partner and said if I would like to join her in the class she would arrange a scholarship. I had no idea who Tamara Daykarhanova was, but I wanted to keep busy at the craft of acting, so I decided to accept the scholarship. This decision changed my world, changed my perception of the theater, and was one of the forces that began to alter American acting styles and theater concepts permanently.

Daykarhanova's studio was a strange world to me. She and the Jilinskys were strict taskmasters. They felt American actors, particularly those trained at the Pasadena Playhouse of the American Academy of Dramatic Arts, had been badly trained. I was told that I had to go through a process of relearning. I was not aware of it then, but at the same time, former American students of Boleslavsky—Lee Strasberg, Stella Adler, and Harold Clurman—had begun teaching classes of their own using similar techniques.

Our teachers said that the American theater was moribund and decadent and that the most of the acting and writing was old fashioned and cliché ridden. They said that the Stanislavskian precepts, practiced at the Art Theater, were the ideal and the basis for the theater of the future. Rosamond and I were deeply impressed and thought we had at last found the way to true theatrical art. We believed that when we learned this way of working, our search would be over and a new world of theater would be miraculously established. Meanwhile, in Russia, former students of Stanislavsky had rejected Stanislavsky and his system as too naturalistic and had joined Meyerhold in forming "a new theater" in Moscow.

During my time of study with the Russians, I saw Pauline Lord perform for the first time. I was afraid to tell anyone at Daykarhanova's about my

Pauline Lord (top) and Laurette Taylor (right), on whom the Russians and the Americans agreed. (Photos courtesy of the John Willis Theatre World/Screen World Archive)

admiration of Pauline Lord's acting because she was, after all, a commercial actress, a Broadway star. So much of the theater is ephemeral. Last night's performance will never be seen in all of its particulars again. It may be relived in memory; but even then, it will certainly be changed by memory. There was a performance, perhaps the greatest that I have ever seen, in which Pauline Lord played Zenobia in Edith Wharton's *Ethan Frome*. In all the years since, I have thought about it at least once a week, trying to recapture what I saw that night. Although the exact details of the performance escape me now, the emotions I felt and the exaltation at having seen great acting remains with me. I was greatly relieved when one of the Russians said that when Stanislavsky was performing in America he had seen only two actresses who knew instinctively everything he had discovered himself about acting: Pauline Lord and Laurette Taylor.

About this time, to help relieve unemployment among actors, playwrights, designers, and other theater workers, the government began the Federal Theatre Project. Hallie Flanagan headed it. Among its most famous productions were *The Living Newspaper* and the Orson Welles and John Houseman collaborations. These productions were rooted in German expressionist theater. The Russians and their disciples were impressed by the theatricality of these productions, but they were critical of the acting.

Despite the presence of the Russians and the Germans in the theaters off-Broadway, Broadway seemed to change very little. The Theatre Guild, the Shuberts, the Gilbert Millers, and the Max Gordons continued to produce their plays written by their in-house playwrights and with their in-house stars in the old, accepted ways. A talented director named Mary Hunter, with the urging of Daykarhanova and the Jilinskys, decided not to wait for Broadway to change, but to start an ensemble acting company that would do plays by American playwrights that Broadway rejected as uncommercial. She started the American Actors Company. The company lasted six years and disbanded when World War II took many of its actors. The company did plays of Paul Green, Lynn Riggs, Ramon Naya, Josephine Nigli, E. P. Conkle, Thornton Wilder, and Arnold Sundgaard, including a musical review, American Legend, directed and choreographed by Agnes de Mille. I was a member of the American Actors Company; and it was as a member of this group that I abandoned acting for writing and had my first plays produced.

Excerpts from Genesis of an American Playwright *by Horton Foote, edited by Marion Castleberry,* © *2004 Baylor University Press, reprinted by permission of Baylor University Press.*

6

······

CHARLES FULLER

Photo by Peter Sumner Walton Bellamy

CHARLES FULLER was born in Philadelphia. He achieved critical notice in 1969 with *The Village: A Party*. He later wrote plays for the Henry Street Settlement Theater and the Negro Ensemble Company in New York. He won an Obie Award for *Zooman and the Sign* in 1980. His next work, *A Soldier's Play*, was a critical success, winning the 1982 Pulitzer Prize. He later adapted the script into the 1984 film *A Soldier's Story*. His screenplay was nominated in 1985 for an Academy Award, a Golden Globe Award, and a Writers Guild of America Award. It won an Edgar Award. Fuller has received grants from the State of New York, the Rockefeller Foundation, the National Endowment for the Arts, and the John Simon Guggenheim Memorial Foundation. He has also written short fiction and screenplays and worked as a movie producer. He is a member of the Writers Guild of America, East.

Memories

(A conversation that took place sometime during the mid-1970s. There had been and would be nearly a dozen or more over a period of fifteen to eighteen years before the writer and essayist Larry Neal died of a heart attack in January of 1981.)

It was between four-thirty and five in the morning when Larry Neal arrived at my door. We lived in a wooded area that had once been a Quaker park, and before the sun rose the place was always a combination of spooky trees dripping with dew and scurrying wildlife racing to daytime shelter ahead of yawning, slow-rising humans. In those days both of my boys were still struggling through adolescence, and a knock at the door at that hour triggered not only their awakening, but the grabbing of baseball bats.

"Who is it, Dad?" they both asked, wiping sleep from their eyes. Charles dragged an aluminum bat and David lofted a mini bat as they followed me down the hallway to the front door.

(I've often wondered how, in lieu of guns, baseball bats have long been thought of—wrongly—as equalizers against breaking and entering attempts or physical assaults. Since most people staging robberies or assaults usually carry guns, getting off a shot is a lot quicker than raising a bat and swinging.)

"Hey, Cholly!" The voice was familiar.

"It's Uncle Larry," I said. Before I released the lock, Charles and David had turned away and were heading for their rooms, mildly disappointed. When the door opened, I heard Charles yawn a greeting.

"Hi, Uncle Larry!"

David simply got back in bed without a sound. My wife never awakened. These visits were all too common—indeed, two or three times a year, Larry and I would be up before dawn, talking over coffee before anyone else arose for work or school.

(We'd known one another since elementary school, and had met when we lived four doors from one another in the James Weldon Johnson Homes—the second "project" for African Americans in North Philly. The Neals lived at 2605-C, the Fullers at 2605-F, Ridge Drive.)

As always, he set his leather briefcase by the door and we moved to the kitchen, where he'd sit down at the table, coat off, hat on, and begin our discussion over hot cups of coffee—and usually some kind of sweet cake—pound, donut, or Danish.

"Cholly, that drive in from Washington is murderous, my brother! I don't think I passed three sane drivers on I-95 from Baltimore to Philly! My question is: 'Must you drive ninety, a hundred miles an hour because you *can*, jeopardizing everybody in *your back seat*, and *we* who have joined you on the road, because *you* have a *jones* about speed? There was an overturned truck and streams of cops and highway cleanup people outside of Wilmington, Delaware, as I drove up. Sad thing was, three—looked like students—college kids, shivering, all wrapped in blankets sitting on the back steps of an ambulance, as the firemen tried to pry somebody they knew out of a steel-gray Pontiac Firebird flipped upside down beneath a tree off the road. It's wasteful, man—like life don't seem to mean a thing!"

He was quiet for a moment.

"Cholly, we need to change some of these things, man!"

"We can't change whether people drive too fast or too slow!"

"I know! But what I'm trying to get to is: we have to believe we can change *some* things—and that art, and specifically writing, is the proper place to create the alternative to what is, and offer that alternative as what can make sense going forward. The accident I saw made me think, man! Check this out. We have been arguing—or let's say jostling with Western ideas about what art is supposed to do since we began expressing ourselves as slaves. We created spirituals, the blues, jazz, R & B—all music, but we changed the beat! It wasn't *country* anymore—hillbilly—quote, unquote, classical, or just religious anymore. Changing the beat, changed what we called the music, and in most instances how *we* felt about it. What if we could do that with the literature?"

"I don't follow—want some more coffee?" I got up and checked the coffee maker.

"Yeah—how are your boys?"

"They brought baseball bats to the front door—to protect me!"

"Can't blame 'em, Cholly—me and Evelyn are talking about—maybe—just maybe, when Avatar *(their son)* reaches high school age, moving out of New York. It's getting nuts on the streets—some places in Harlem are getting like North Philly *used* to be!"

I poured another cup of coffee and set it on the table.

"I always did like this circular table, man."

"It's getting old—what about the literature?"

"Yeah—like I was saying: Do you drive ninety or a hundred, just because you *can*—and endanger everyone on the highway, including yourself? Or do you shift to a lower speed—or maybe not drive on the highway at all? Maybe try an alternative route—more scenic, less traveled—and not necessarily because it's safer, but because the *highway* makes you do things—habits—that over time, make you think less about your safety, and more about speed? Take Western literature—or better still, English. We speak it, write it, study it, and generally, as a consequence, measure how well we work in it by the ideas of people who made English *their* car. They also over time, built the highway on which that car has to drive. They set the speed limit, the point at which the highway began, laid out its direction, drew the maps, and, to a great extent, Cholly, decided what the *best* English should *look* like, *feel* like, and *sound* like, once it reached the destination *they* set for it! The question I ask them is why is that highway good just because you set its direction? What if we have something to say that doesn't necessarily fit into the *look*, *feel*, and *sound* you think English ought to have? Can we still call it English? And if, in the way that all language does, it gets you to where you need to go—understanding—haven't we reached our destination, even though you didn't draw the route?"

He sipped at his coffee.

"The literature is the only form we had kept—essentially, the way the West gave it to us, Cholly! From the slave narratives until the black arts movement—in the essay, novel, poetry, and playwriting, we've always used the rules handed down to us—notwithstanding an occasional flourish in content—say, Dunbar's poetry, Ellison's *Invisible Man*, Hansberry's *A Raisin in the Sun*, Chesnutt's 'The Wife of His Youth,' Cruse's *The Crisis of the Negro Intellectual*—but until we changed the focus during the black arts movement, the language hadn't changed!"

"I'm not understanding, Larry."

The voice came from down the hall.

"Hi, Larry—how's Evelyn?" It was my wife.

"She's fine—been swearing she's going to get down here to see y'all!"

"Right!" The bathroom door closed behind her.

"Oops! Guess I blew that!"

"Big time! But what are you driving at—get back to this literature thing—and English."

"Dig it! Ask yourself, Cholly, what is the major purpose of language? What does language do more than anything else? Check this out. *(Here he began to point.)* It allows us to communicate and define—ideas, directions, wants, feelings—everything about ourselves and the world around us and—in the process of doing so, preserve *our culture and its place on the world stage*. The terms that define our history, our heroes and traitors, our future, our past, our goods and evils—who's favored and who's not—intelligent or dumb, our gods and angels are all part of the business of our language. Now, if English is that car—just suppose we point it in another direction? Arrive at another destination? Or take another road, and by doing so, add dimension and fullness to American culture and hence change the look of this country's place on the world stage—like for example—elect a black president?"

I laughed out loud. "You dreamin', Larry!"

"Probably—but it would change the language—overthrow our understanding of leadership."

"Maybe, but remember, you said that the change could be brought about through the literature, 'that art and specifically, writing, is the proper place to create the alternative to what is, and offer that alternative as what can make sense going forward.' I'll tell you what we can do right now—what about *messing* with the literature?"

"What do you mean? Any more coffee?"

"A whole pot." I got up as my wife left the bathroom.

"You know, you two wake up the whole house," she said. I could hear her slippers sliding across the floor before the bedroom door shut loudly.

"Never did hold her tongue, did she? Thought I'd forget? Remember, I was in the wedding party, my man! What about *messing* with the King's language?"

I filled the cup again and sat back down.

"Thanks. I'm 'a need this on the road, that Jersey Turnpike's a sleep-inducing bitch, Cholly! Anyway . . . "

"It's not so much about the language," I hesitated, "but you now this thing I'm researching? 'Bout the Second World War? And black soldiers?"

"Yeah."

"I've been thinking—and I'm not sure yet, but I'd like to mess with the literature and the history."

"Ain't much you can do with the history—it is what it is."

"That depends on who's looking and from what angle, Larry."

"OK. But on that literature tip you might have something, Cholly— I've been trying to find an American piece of literature that I can take and completely turn it around, upside down and inside out. The way everybody does with Brecht's *Mother Courage* . . . except that you don't do it in another time frame or American setting—you take it and you flip it—make it something completely different—something black, but its heart—its spine is a piece of American literature—a well-known piece of American lit."

"A well-known piece of American lit . . . A well-known piece of American lit."

(Larry left the house around eleven in the morning on his way back to New York. Shortly thereafter he would work in Washington, D.C., as that city's arts director.)

I wouldn't begin writing *A Soldier's Play* for another four or five years. I wrote a musical about Ethel Waters that no one liked—worked with the Negro Ensemble Company, where we did a play called *Zooman and the Sign* and shortly thereafter read Herman Melville's *Billy Budd*. It was a third reading. As one of Melville's shorter pieces, it fit the need I had to take my mind off how I would begin writing a new play—like a lot of writers, I was close to being broke, and more than anything I needed to calm down and stop worrying about where I'd find my next dollar. Easier said then done— but the more I worried, the farther away I got from being able to create— anything! Before I began reading Melville, however, I got a call from Evelyn Neal. Toward eleven at night, in January of 1981.

"Charlie, this is Evelyn. Larry died of a heart attack this evening—after dinner. He was at Wesleyan."

Left to right: Brent Jennings, Steven Jones, Eugene Lee, Denzel Washington, Samuel L. Jackson, James Pickens Jr., and Peter Friedman in the 1981 Negro Ensemble Company production of Charles Fuller's A Soldier's Play *at Theatre Four. (Photo reprinted by permission of the estate of Bert Andrews, courtesy of the John Willis Theatre World/Screen World Archive)*

I remember the day of the funeral, sitting speechless in Larry's basement with some of the finest writers in America and no one knowing quite what to do—or say. Everyone there was a friend. We all knew, I believe, that our silence only reflected the silence Harlem and a chunk of American lit would experience without Larry's voice.

In the pages of *Billy Budd* I found what I needed—an American classic and something that, if I turned it inside out and upside down, would be exactly what Larry Neal and I had discussed. With that in mind, it didn't take long to write the play. Before it was finished, however, my father died on the Fourth of July, Independence Day.

What I knew about *A Soldier's Play* before I gave it to Douglas Turner Ward and the Negro Ensemble Company was that it worked, because Melville's story had worked, and that I had accomplished what Larry and I had discussed that evening during the 1970s. Whether it would change behavior I couldn't be sure, but I had successfully taken a piece of American lit and turned it inside out and upside down and emerged with something brand new—something that, as luck would have it, changed my life.

7

......

A. R. GURNEY

A. R. "Pete" Gurney has been writing plays for many years. Among them are *The Dining Room, The Cocktail Hour, Love Letters, Sylvia, Far East, Ancestral Voices, Big Bill, Mrs. Farnsworth, Indian Blood,* and *Buffalo Gal.* He has also written three novels, several television scripts, and librettos for operas. Gurney was recently inducted into the Theatre Hall of Fame and the American Academy of Arts and Letters. He has honorary degrees from Williams College and Buffalo State College and taught literature at the Massachusetts Institute for Technology for many years.

Back in Buffalo

I don't believe there was any one play that influenced my decision to write for the theatre. Rather, it was theatre in general which set me on the path to sin, shame, and uncertain glory. I grew up in Buffalo, New York, as I probably have announced too many times, and at that time it seemed I was surrounded with plays. We were always acting in school plays and watching others perform in them. Furthermore, our parents were up to the same sort of thing. Buffalo was, and still is, a clubby sort of town, so at an early age I was taken to my mother's luncheon and bridge club, where I saw her sing "Thanks for the Memories" in a red dress and forget the words. My father's club, which was a few blocks farther downtown, also put on shows, but they were deemed "a little old" for me. My father made it clear, however, that his club's theatrical endeavors, especially when they followed his suggestions, were much more amusing than those of my mother.

Yet much of the material I played in or saw performed during those years wasn't just kid's stuff or in-house skits. I saw my older sister play the Lady in her school's production of Milton's masque *Comus,* which was elaborately staged out-of-doors in an opulent local garden. I saw my brother play a gypsy

Godfrey Tearle as Antony and Katharine Cornell as Cleopatra in the 1947 Broadway production of William Shakespeare's Antony and Cleopatra *at the Martin Beck Theatre. (Photo courtesy of Photofest)*

in some Austrian operetta where he urged my second cousin to run off with him: "O, what care I," he sang, "for a goose-feather bed." The Junior League of Buffalo had somehow acquired a magnificent set of marionettes that they used to present a series of Greek and Roman myths at yet another club. There were also plenty of performances of Gilbert and Sullivan by the upper grades of our various schools, and while my family didn't go to church much, we always made a point of seeing the annual Christmas pageant at Trinity Church.

Not far from where we lived was the Studio Theatre, a *semi-professional* organization, run by a passionate devotee of dramatic art named Jane Keeler, who reproduced Broadway hits by meticulously following the ground plans and stage directions published in the Samuel French playbooks. Many of my parents' friends performed for Miss Keeler in works like *Ah, Wilderness!* or *Knickerbocker Holiday*, and many of the girls my age took acting classes there to improve their Buffalo accents. Topping things off was the Erlanger Theatre, placed at the foot of our stately Delaware Avenue, in a much prouder location than the many movie theatres clustered one block over on Main Street. At the Erlanger, we could see touring productions coming from New York or heading in that general direction. Many of us had grandmothers who subscribed to the season's offerings by the Theatre Guild, and if you showed any kind of interest and had no hopes of going skiing that Saturday, these elegant ladies might take us to a matinee where we could see the opulent red curtain rise on Katharine Cornell being gracious and sacrificial in *The Barretts of Wimpole Street*, or Paul Robeson being systematically destroyed by José Ferrer in *Othello*, or even a tryout of a play called *Summer and Smoke* on its way to Broadway by that daring new playwright named Tennessee Williams.

Several times a year my parents would take the train down to what they called "fabulous New York." My father did real estate business there, but I had the sense that theatregoing was their prime objective. On their last night in New York, they'd have the bellboy from their hotel deliver their bags to their stateroom on a Pullman car on the Empire State Express at Grand Central Station, so they could see one more play before they jumped aboard. They'd usually meet people they knew in the club car, where they'd discuss what they had seen all the way up the Hudson River to Albany. Then they'd go to bed and wake up in Buffalo. Afterward, my parents would tell me what plays they had seen and who was in them, and so I grew up hearing about the Lunts, and Gertrude Lawrence, and Walter Huston, and how exciting they all were onstage.

Television didn't exist then, but radio did, with a vengeance. If I got my homework done, I was allowed to listen to plays presented over the air: "This is Cecil B. DeMille for the *Lux Radio Theatre*. . . ." And there were many more theatres on the air, introduced by announcers who would pretend they were taking us to a real theatre: "Now the houselights dim and the silver curtain rises on the first act of. . . ." There were also excellent dramas, like *I Love a Mystery* or *Suspense*, which were written especially for the radio medium and capitalized on creepy auditory effects. I suspect that by listening to all of these programs I learned subliminally how to tell a story primarily through dialogue. Harold Pinter called the BBC dramatic broadcasts a major influence on his writing, and I imagine those American playwrights who grew up on radio owe that medium a similar debt.

In any case, I was bitten by the theatre bug in Buffalo at an early age and have remained infected ever since. When a composition was assigned in class, I usually asked if I could write a play instead. Occasionally I was even allowed to, and shamelessly worked for the laughs I might get if I could read my piece aloud in class. Perhaps my parents sensed that I was starting down a very dangerous path because they sent me away to a boys' boarding school, where I immediately joined the theatre organization and played the female lead in *The Man Who Came to Dinner*. The horny audience hooted and cheered when I came onstage, and nicknamed me "Legs Gurney" when I got off—an experience which was so humiliating that I gave up acting forever.

In my senior year at boarding school, I got special permission to take the train all the way down to New York to see Katharine Cornell in *Antony and Cleopatra*. We had been studying the play in English class, and I persuaded the teacher that I'd learn something by seeing it played onstage, especially by the First Lady of the American Stage, who, of course, came from Buffalo. My grandmother wrote her a note saying I hoped to stop by afterward, so back I went, where she sat me down and offered me a Coca-Cola. As I remember it now, I told her more about Buffalo than she told me about Shakespeare, but I learned, amid the backstage bustle around me, that theatre was hard work and not just fun and games. I've recently written a play called *The Grand Manner* that amplifies this experience.

At Williams College, I was very much influenced by the accomplishments of Stephen Sondheim, who was two classes ahead of me and light years beyond me in talent and experience. While he was there, he bravely changed the nature of the traditional college spring musical. He threw out the silly parody plots, and cast women from Smith and Bennington to supplant the usual all-male hairy-legged kick choruses. When he graduated, his distinguished mantle fell heavily on my puny shoulders. I couldn't sustain a story, but I could write a skit or two and a lyric which aspired to rhyme. I signed up for a music course, enlisted several of my friends, and somehow we came up something we called "a sophisticated revue," comforting ourselves with the fact that New York was doing it, too, with such shows as *Lend an Ear* or *Two on the Aisle*. My senior year at Williams, I had the choice of writing an honors thesis on *The Winter's Tale* or doing another student musical. So, in my desperate attempt to contrive a plot, I proposed we do a musical adaptation of Shaw's *Pygmalion*. The director of drama rejected the idea as hopeless, and told me to concentrate on my thesis. I did, but I also found time to organize a second revue as well, and to persuade my classmate George Steinbrenner to play one of the two pianos to accompany our songs.

The Korean War was beginning to wind down in 1952 when I graduated, but the draft was full upon us, so I signed up for Officer Candidate School at Newport, Rhode Island, which committed me to three and a half years in the Navy. I was assigned to the giant aircraft carrier *Franklin D. Roosevelt*, which was prowling around the Mediterranean, showing the flag, and boasting a large ship's band to play our national anthem and that of our various host countries. The theatre bug was still very much in my system, so I wrote and directed another musical revue, to be performed in the ship's huge hangar deck, with the front elevator partially raised to serve as a stage. The ship's complement of almost five thousand provided considerable talent, and the ship's band capably accompanied them. We were a huge success for our captive audience, but at the end of the show, we had to strike our limited set very quickly to accommodate the ship's boxing matches.

After I was mustered out of the Navy, I was admitted to the Yale School of Drama. There I wrote several short pieces which were published in the annual *Best American Short Plays* series, and sold a play to the *Schlitz Television Theatre*. I also wrote the book and lyrics for a show called *Love in Buffalo*, which was the first musical that the drama school had ever produced, and the libretto for a musical of *Tom Sawyer* which was performed at the gigantic Kansas City Starlight Theatre. But by the time I graduated from the drama school in 1958, I was married, with our first child well on the way, and I felt in my bones that I had told the world everything I had to say.

It is obvious that plays were very much a part of the general cultural life all during that time. Arthur Miller, Tennessee Williams, and William Inge were flexing their muscles on Broadway, and those of us who had any talent at all saw the possibility of a future in the theatre. That said, I spent the next twenty-five years of my life in academia and in helping to raise my four children. I had lucked into a temporary job teaching literature in the Humanities Department at MIT, and as the department grew, I managed to grow with it. Talking about Aeschylus or Dante or Faulkner to classes of unusually bright students whose first commitments were to science and engineering, and who had been up late the night before doing problem sets and lab reports, enabled me to develop a particular kind of stand-up technique for dealing with the material. I developed my own courses, and I learned that teaching itself can be a kind of performance. In any case, I managed somehow to keep at least a good part of my audiences awake and interested. While I taught, my love of conventional theatre took hold again, as a kind of sideline. With a group of actors and writers, we started our own company in Boston—called the New Theatre for Now—and we put on our short plays in a South End coffee house. You could say that for those long years I was a teacher who wrote, secretly yearning to be a writer who taught. Finally, in 1982, after almost twenty-five years in harness, under pressure from my wife and with my play *The Dining Room* beginning to bring in some extra money, we moved to New York. I commuted to MIT for several years afterward, but for all practical purposes I became a full-time writer of plays.

Looking back, I should add that there were a number of plays, or rather productions of plays, which I see now as stepping-stones toward a life more committed to the theatre. The musical *Annie Get Your Gun,* which I saw on my first trip to New York, indelibly impressed on me the excitement and pace of a good evening in the theatre, where you could actually have something going on in front of a curtain while you changed the scenery behind it. Elia Kazan's production of *A Streetcar Named Desire* taught me how a good set and a good sound system can take a terrific play to a higher level. Uta Hagen's production of Shaw's *Saint Joan* at the New York City Center showed me how a play could be intellectually thrilling and profoundly moving at the same time. Tyrone Guthrie's production of Thornton Wilder's *The Matchmaker* demonstrated how a savvy playwright, director, and actors can put their arms around an audience and lead it gently into a special world where they can accept all sorts of fanciful turns of the plot and be thoroughly amused by the process. The plays of Harold Pinter, especially *The Homecoming,* were lessons in stage silences and mysteries of plot which could remain unsolved at the end. And Peter Brook's production of *Marat/Sade* showed me that you could aggressively call attention to the artificiality and limitations of the stage and still hold an audience in a tight grip.

Interestingly enough, the plays that you'd think might have influenced me strongly—comedies of manners like *The Philadelphia Story* or the works of Noël Coward or Somerset Maugham—didn't make much of an impression when I first read or saw them, though I appreciate them more now. Finally, even though I came lately to New York, I was lured on by the successes of other American playwrights who were making a splash at that time. As

Clockwise from top: Terence Rigby, Michael Craig, Paul Rogers, John Normington, Ian Holm, and Vivien Merchant in the 1967 Broadway production of Harold Pinter's The Homecoming *at the Music Box Theatre. (Photo courtesy of the John Willis Theatre World/Screen World Archive)*

the mainstream Broadway theatre was beginning to branch out into various smaller Off-Broadway rivulets, I noticed that Shepard, Mamet, McNally, Kopit, and Durang, to name just a few, were all exploring new territories with energy and inventiveness. While I was older than most of them and a latecomer to the party, I discovered that I also had a subject and a territory, namely the world I grew up in and how it was responding to these changing times. The people I wanted to write about hadn't appeared onstage for quite a while and seemed ripe for plucking. So I staked my claim in that particular area, and for better or worse have been exploring the many customs and facets of the haute bourgeoisie de Beau Fleuve pretty much ever since.

8

......

BETH HENLEY

BETH HENLEY was born in Jackson, Mississippi. Her plays have been produced internationally and translated into over ten languages. *Crimes of the Heart* (The Golden Theatre) and *The Wake of Jamey Foster* (Eugene O'Neill Theatre) were performed on Broadway. Off-Broadway productions include *The Miss Firecracker Contest, Am I Blue, The Lucky Spot, The Debutante Ball, Abundance, Impossible Marriage,* and *Family Week.* Her play *Ridiculous Fraud* was recently produced at McCarter Theatre as well as South Coast Repertory Theatre. Henley's newest work, *The Jacksonian,* had a staged reading in the summer of 2009 at New York Stage and Film.

Henley was awarded the Pulitzer Prize in Drama and the New York Drama Critics' Circle Award for Best American Play for *Crimes of the Heart.* Her other awards include: American Theatre Wing 1998 Award for Distinguished Achievement in Playwriting, and she was a finalist for the Susan Smith Blackburn Prize for *Crimes of the Heart* and *Ridiculous Fraud.* She was a New York Stage and Film honoree in 2007.

Henley wrote the screenplay for the acclaimed film version of *Crimes of the Heart,* for which she was nominated for an Academy Award. The film was directed by Bruce Beresford and starred Diane Keaton, Jessica Lange, Sissy Spacek, and Sam Shepard. She also wrote the screenplay for *Miss Firecracker,* starring Holly Hunter and Tim Robbins. She wrote the screenplay for *Nobody's Fool,* which starred Rosanna Arquette and Eric Roberts, and co-wrote David Byrne's *True Stories.* Her television credits include *Surviving Love,* a film for CBS starring Ted Danson and Mary Steenburgen, as well as a teleplay for the PBS series *Trying Times,* directed by Jonathan Demme.

Henley has the honor of serving as Theater Arts Presidential Professor at Loyola Marymount University in Los Angeles. She is a board member of the Fellowship of Southern Writers and serves on the PEN/Faulkner Writers Advisory Council.

Plays That Changed My Life

It wasn't a play that initially entranced me with the theatre. It was the day my mother arrived to pick up the kindergarten carpool painted green. Astonished, the children and teachers crowded around our station wagon marveling at the green being behind the wheel. Mama was playing the Green Bean Man in a children's theatre production of *Jack and the Beanstalk*. Maybe she was coming from a dress rehearsal, because she was late and in a hurry. Being very thin and sprightly, she made a dashing Green Bean Man. How thrilled I was by her transformation from my mother to a green elf. She had eclipsed species *and* gender.

The magic faded when I saw the play. The Beautiful Princess was a hunched-over, disgruntled, word-swallowing MISTAKE. Why was *she* playing the fair young damsel? My disappointment was catastrophic. I wanted to get lost in the world of giants, magic beans, poor people, and gold. But I could not suspend disbelief long enough to stop believing that the princess should have been cast as the giant or, better yet, a non-speaking peasant. Thus, from an early age, I recognized that casting was crucial. It could make or break a production, and a good actor was hard to find.

Not long after *Beanstalk* (I was learning that theatre people never said the whole name of a play, which let you know they *were* theatre people) I went with my father and sisters to pick Mama up after the last matinee of *Rain* (*A Hatful of Rain* to "civilians").

When we arrived, big men were knocking down the room that was onstage. They frightened me with their big knocking-down equipment and terrible shouts. The sad-looking room was being torn apart like there was no tomorrow. Walls crashed, sawdust flew, cabinets were ruthlessly ripped away.

I found my mother standing in the wings distraught and weeping. I asked her what was wrong.

"They're tearing down our home. My kitchen."

"Why?"

"Because we've closed, Pinkie. We've closed."

I wondered why they had to get rid of it all so fast.

"Couldn't they leave it a day or two? A little longer?"

"No. They have to strike so they can load in another show. They'll be here all night."

And then she was wiping away tears and going to joke with all the loud, awful men who were hacking down the walls of her home.

I was angry and mixed up, but on some level I learned that the theatre is real, very real, and then it ends. A whole world is created that will never stay. How could grown-up people work so hard on something that they knew would disappear in a flash? But I saw these plays were important to my mother in a way real life wasn't. Garden-club prizes, grocery shopping, building our patio, or bringing cupcakes to school did not compare to being in the theatre. And it never would.

I can't remember the first play I saw my mother acting in, but one that stands out is Jean Kerr's *Mary, Mary* (aka *Mary*). This play made a lasting impression because it taught me about "quick changes" and "stage kisses." Mama was playing the lead, Mary; and Mary wore a lot of clothes. Very sophisticated Eastern clothes, perfectly accessorized and exotically wintry. There was fur. Lots and lots of fur. Fur-lined boots, gloves, sweaters, and hats. It was all glamorous and sparkling and very funny when people talked about divorce.

Behind a flat there was a small corner where my mother had to take off one entire costume and put on another in a matter of seconds. She had two dressers to help her and the operation was breathtakingly precise. One flubbed second and she would miss her cue.

One of the most exciting moments of the show for me was when Mary took her exit for the quick change and I knew she was rushing like a house afire to get her clothes off and on, and then, as soon as the lights changed, she was there, calm and cool, in a whole new ensemble, lighting a cigarette.

The other part of the play that intrigued and deeply shocked me was when my mother was kissed by a handsome, elegant man on a couch.

She explained it wasn't really a kiss. It was a "stage kiss."

I wasn't convinced. Why couldn't they just turn their heads away from the audience and rub cheeks? The way they were doing it, their lips touched and the audience might mistake it for a real kiss. I told Mama that it did not bother me because I understood it was acting, but:

"What about Daddy? Won't he be upset?"

"No, of course not. He knows Clive doesn't like women."

"Oh."

Clive was always nice to me and I knew he and my mother were crazy about each other. But the way she said "Clive doesn't like women" made me know something I did not know. I stopped worrying that my parents were going to divorce over the "stage kiss." Even if people's lips touched, it was all make-believe. There were things you could do in the theatre that would not be allowed anywhere else. I became a devotee.

The delight I got from theatre expressions was profound. It was a secret language, a gypsy jive:

Ken Evans as the gentleman caller and Lydy Becker Caldwell (Beth Henley's mother) as Laura Wingfield in the 1966 production of Tennessee Williams' The Glass Menagerie *at New Stage Theatre in Jackson, Mississippi. (Photo courtesy of New Stage Theatre)*

Cast Party, BYOB, understudy, upstaging, phoning it in, salmon gel, two-hander, no royalties, goddamn critics, the Scottish play, building costumes, half hour, cue light, callbacks, green room, glow tape, blocking, blackout, Places! ghost light . . .

I would often help my mother memorize lines. We would lie up on her big four-poster bed and go over her part until she was "word perfect." I knew to skip the long speeches of the other characters and go right to her "cue." She never became exasperated when I corrected her, only when I didn't. Mama liked to get "off book" in the first week of rehearsal. She could do this because she was a "quick study."

"Memory is a muscle, Pinkie. The more you memorize the more you can remember."

This was heartening to me, in that memorizing was all I seemed to be doing at Duling Elementary School: "Memorize all the states, the state capitals, the state flowers, and the state birds. Memorize all of the counties in Mississippi and be able to recite them in alphabetical order. If you omit any county you will have to start over at the beginning until you do it correctly."

Even more miserable was staying after school to work on my cramped handwriting and writing over and over again all the words I misspelled over and over again.

My big chance to escape civilian life came when the Jackson Little Theatre decided to include the prologue in their production of *Summer and Smoke*. It is a short scene between Young Miss Alma and Young John at the stone angel's fountain.

My mother let me audition because if I got the part I could do the scene, go home, get up for school, and forgo the curtain call except on weekends. She did not want me to fall behind in school or become an obnoxious child actor.

Auditions were fraught. Mama warned me I wasn't typecast for the willowy, sickly Young Alma. My allergy doctor remarked that I was the only overweight asthmatic he had ever treated.

But fate, or the fact that Mama was running props and was willing to bring me every night, prevailed and I got the part!

When my costume measurements were taken, I sucked in my stomach, held my breath, and pretended to smile. Costumes were ordered from a New York stock costume company. When my old-fashioned, girlie dress arrived I was giddy beyond Easter shoes and parasols. Mama felt (and rightly so, as Williams' instructions call for a "middy blouse") the costume was too floozy and a preacher's daughter wouldn't wear such a thing. She preferred something more tailored—a crisply pressed sailor suit.

I begged not to wear a sailor suit. I wanted the frilly costume from the New York stock costume company. Mama looked at my desperate face and relented.

After all, there were other difficulties. I immediately went on the Metracal diet, where I was allowed four cans of chocolate-flavored liquid a day. Determined to look sickly ethereal, I drank the undrinkable stuff without complaint.

Not focused on my figure, the director was concerned because I was mumbling my words. My breathy voice could not be heard even when he exclaimed:

"Louder, Little Alma! We can't hear you past the footlights! Louder, for God's sake!"

At home Mama had me shout all my lines while holding a pencil clutched between my teeth. Although my sisters groaned and ridiculed, this extra training helped. Eventually, when I spoke my lines without a pencil in my mouth, there was a marked improvement in my projection as well as my enunciation.

I wore a fake braid so Young John could pull the ribbon to tease me as he left stage. We would put the fake braid on at home. Boxes of bobby pins were jammed into my scalp, almost nailing the braid to my skull. Once I had the braid on, all I needed to do at the theatre was put on my costume and check my props.

"Always check your own props, Pinkie. It's your responsibility. Actors who don't check their own props are amateurs or fools."

Dress rehearsal night my father was staying home with my sisters. When I was leaving for the theatre he wished me well.

"Have a good show, Little Buddy. And don't get stage fright."

"What's stage fright?"

Mama gave Daddy a look.

"There's no such thing as stage fright. He made that up."

"Break a leg," my father offered.

"I will!"

It was like a dream being in a production with real adult actors. Miss Alma, played by Jane Petty, was a vision with her pale skin, clear blue eyes, and steady gaze.

She taught me to shut my eyes tightly as soon as I turned upstage at the end of the scene. That way my vision could adjust enough so that I could make my way offstage in the blackout. Emulating Jane Petty, I would twist the ring on my finger around and around. How well the gesture revealed Miss

Alma's otherworldliness, her nervous sensitivity. I wondered if Jane Petty was my doppelgänger.

Things went wonderfully until the night Scott Cook (Young John) pulled my hair ribbon with such force that the fake braid came flying off my head and was left clutched in his fist.

After banging offstage in the blackout, I ran tearfully down a hallway to hide my humiliation. Scott got yelled at by a grown-up and he was sent after me to apologize. He promised he was sorry.

"I only pulled it hard once, to see what would happen."

I nodded my head, pretending to be fine.

"I won't do it again."

We stood silently in the dark hall.

There was a moment in the scene where Young John quickly kisses young Alma on the cheek. Scott pondered what it would be like to kiss for real? On the mouth?

I wondered as well.

We kissed on the lips in the dark hallway.

I ran away. Heart pounding, believing my reputation was forever ruined because I had kissed on the lips while only in fifth grade elementary.

Kisses seemed to be a theme in the theatre. I imagined with rehearsal I could get used to them.

My final and complete rebellion against "civilian life" came when I learned I would not be allowed to see the play that was opening the New Stage Theatre. A small church down by the railroad tracks had been converted into a fifty-seat theatre. It was going to be Jackson's first *experimental* theatre. The town was in an uproar because their premiere production was Edward Albee's *Who's Afraid of Virginia Woolf?* Now I had no idea who Edward Albee or Virginia Woolf was, but I wanted to see something *experimental*.

I asked my mother, "What is so bad about Virginia Woolf?"

"It's a play on words. Who's afraid of the big bad wolf? Who's afraid of Virginia Woolf? How people fear knowing the truth. All that we hide. Fear and lies."

I did not get it. On further study I learned Virginia Woolf was an English writer who put rocks in her pockets and walked into a river so she could drown. What was so scary about that? Why did you have to be seventeen to get into that?

My mother didn't mind if I saw the play, but she didn't want to rock the boat. The theatre was already under fire for being avant-garde. They were opening with a play that used profanity, dealt with sexual subjects, and was

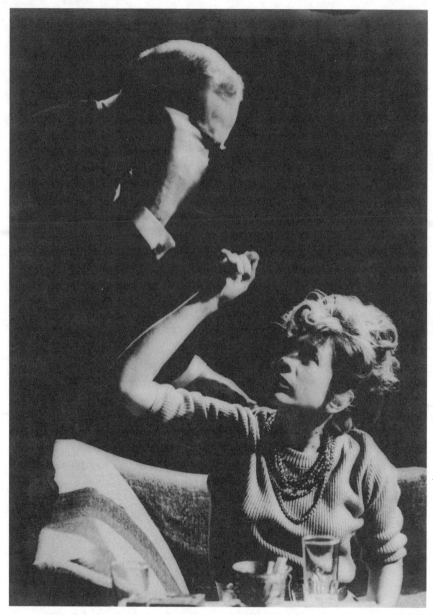

Frank Hains as George and Jane Reid Petty as Martha in the 1965 production of Edward Albee's Who's Afraid of Virginia Woolf? *at the New Stage Theatre in Jackson, Mississippi. (Photo courtesy of New Stage Theatre)*

written by a homosexual. All of this, on top of the fact that Negroes were welcome to buy tickets and be audience members.

Damn, I wanted to see that play. I picked up a copy of *Woolf* that we had around the house and read it diligently, like I knew what it was about, and could not understand why the "civilians" were so outraged. The play is, after all, art. Absolutely, in my estimation, it was fine art and these small-minded objections were stupid and entirely despicable.

Really. *"Who's Afraid of Virginia Woolf?"* Who?!

Well, I wasn't.

The theatre wasn't.

And neither was my mama.

9

......

TINA HOWE

Photo by Tom Bloom

TINA HOWE's plays include *The Nest, Birth and After Birth, Museum, The Art of Dining, Painting Churches, Coastal Disturbances, Approaching Zanzibar, One Shoe Off, Pride's Crossing, Such Small Hands, Rembrandt's Gift,* and new translations of Eugène Ionesco's *The Bald Soprano* and *The Lesson,* as well as a host of shorter plays. These works premiered at the New York Shakespeare Festival, the Kennedy Center, Second Stage Theatre, the Old Globe Theatre, Lincoln Center Theater, the Actors Theatre of Louisville, and the Atlantic Theater Company. Her most recent play, *Chasing Manet,* opened at Primary Stages in the spring of 2009. Among her many awards are an Obie for Distinguished Playwriting, a Tony nomination for Best Play, an Outer Critics Circle Award, a Rockefeller grant, two NEA Fellowships, a Guggenheim Fellowship, the American Academy of Arts and Letters Award in Literature, the Dramatists Guild Fund Madge Evans/Sidney Kingsley Award for Outstanding Achievement in the Theatre, the New York Drama Critics' Circle Award, two honorary degrees, and the William Inge Award for Distinguished Achievement in the American Theatre. Twice a finalist for the Pulitzer Prize, Howe has been a visiting professor at Hunter College since 1990 and has also taught master classes at New York University, UCLA, Columbia University, and Carnegie Mellon University. Her works can be read in numerous anthologies as well as in *Coastal Disturbances: Four Plays by Tina Howe, Approaching Zanzibar and Other Plays* (both Theatre Communications Group), and most recently her translations of Ionesco's *The Bald Soprano* and *The Lesson* (Grove Press). Howe is proud to have served on the council of the Dramatists Guild of America since 1990.

"Tiens, il est neuf heures"

Hunched over the twelfth draft of the dreadful short story I was trying to finish before graduation, I finally had to face the fact that I wasn't a fiction writer. "Worst in class" had already been rubber-stamped onto my forehead, so my teacher wasn't surprised when I threw in the towel. But what to do? I had to turn in *something*! So I did what any normal Sarah Lawrence girl would do: I decided to write a play instead. The fact that I'd never studied theatre or taken a class in playwriting didn't deter me. On the contrary. I thought, "This will be perfect! I won't have to write a word! I'll just put some characters on stage and they'll write it for me!"

Which is just what they did, offering up a dizzy end-of-the-world meditation about waiting. The action took place by a dying stream as an abandoned queen roamed the countryside looking for her cheating husband, accompanied by a chorus of pigeons cawing nonsense and molting feathers onto the desolation below. Jane Alexander, my dear friend and classmate and star of every college production, was charmed by my brazen voice and insisted on producing it. The year was 1959. A student-written work had never been presented before, but when the theatre department heard Jane wanted to direct it, they immediately gave it a green light, and we were off.

She dragged three stepladders onto the stage and rehearsed our chorus of pigeons, giving them the style and foreboding of a Greek tragedy. And best of all, when the leading lady suddenly fell ill on opening night, she took over!

With Jane at the helm, the performance was a triumph—with endless curtain calls and a standing ovation! When the cry "Author! Author!" went up, I rushed onstage and started blowing kisses to the audience, which included my speechless fiction teacher! I was finally pulled off by the proverbial hook, but the die had been cast! I wasn't going to write the great American novel, but the great American play!

The day after graduation my father gave me the following choice: "I'll either send you to graduate school or Europe for a year; which would you prefer?"

Three months later Jane and I were on a student ship chugging across the Atlantic. We both had our covers in place. She was going to study mathematics at the University of Edinburgh, and I was going to study philosophy at the Sorbonne. Within a month Jane was acting in the fringe and I was hard at work on my first full-length play. I found a small room on the top floor of the City Hotel at the tip of the Île de la Cité, overlooking the Seine and Pont Neuf. It cost a mere $60 a month. So what if the bathroom was down the hall and the one shower in the building was four floors below and cost twenty francs? I'd landed in paradise. I stopped going to classes at the Sorbonne.

Talk about being a cliché of an American in Paris. . . . When I walked down the street, the French would scream with laughter, crying, "Voilà, la Tour Eiffel!," so I hung out with English and American writers. It was an Englishman who took me to the play that would change my life forever— Eugène Ionesco's *La cantatrice chauve*.

Never having studied theatre, I had no idea who Ionesco or the Absurdists were, so I walked into the tiny Théâtre de la Huchette not knowing what to expect. But the moment those deadpan actors started spouting nonsense, I was home! And I mean *literally* home, with my high-minded parents, who read us the classics on weekdays but then took us to the Marx Brothers' double bills on the weekend, laughing themselves liquid and worse. It was all so *familiar*!

The anarchy . . .

Delirium . . .

Hilarity . . .

And all performed with utter *sang froid* as the words that were spoken kept flying out of control.

Finally! I was seeing my first realistic play! And in French! Which is such a chewy language to begin with—like speaking with mouthful of caramel corn. Just say this quickly and you'll hear what I mean: "Tiens, il est neuf heures. Nous avons mangé de la soupe, du poisson, des pommes de terre au lard, de la salade anglaise. . . ."

Ionesco was not only celebrating the tragedy of language, but the courage it takes to communicate at all! Suddenly my course was clear. I would dramatize *female* ritual through a similar lens, exploring the ways *we* struggle to express ourselves.

Foolish girl!

If critics and artistic directors had problems with Absurdism handled by the fellas, you can imagine how they responded to me. My early plays either closed in a night or never saw the light of day, so I took off my clown suit. No more hijinks *inside* of plays. I'd focus on their *containers* instead, taking on unlikely settings like museums, restaurants, beaches, and nursing homes. It was time for elegance, spaciousness, surprise—audiences wiggling their toes in twenty tons of sand at *Coastal Disturbances* at Circle in the Square—or the lights coming up inside a whitewashed nursing home where suspended wheelchairs cast eerie shadows on the walls in *Chasing Manet*.

The weight and dimensions of my work would now be determined by where it took place. Or to put it another way, I'd capture the audience with

The marquee of the Théâtre de la Huchette in Paris, where Eugène Ionesco's La cantatrice chauve (The Bald Soprano) *has been playing for over fifty years. (Photo by Tina Howe)*

the *range* of my imagination, setting plays in swimming pools, dentists' offices, subway cars, and even beneath the World Trade Center when Philippe Petit took his extraordinary stroll on a cable rigged between the Twin Towers in the summer of 1974. No more frisky behavior under the kitchen sink; it was time for broader horizons.

My directors and set designers loved it!

Jack O'Brien had to stage an out-of-control croquet game in *Pride's Crossing* at Lincoln Center's Mitzi Newhouse Theater. There were no wickets and no balls, only a group of elderly players swinging their mallets. His solution was brilliant. The moment their mallets made contract with the invisible ball, the stage manager would cue a *thwok* sound, so the game could disintegrate into a delirious madhouse with everyone playing at once. Isn't that the point of drama, after all? To whip an audience into a frenzy of delight?

When twenty-five actors were performing *Disorderly Conduct* at Town Hall, on the one-year anniversary of the attack on the World Trade Center, all they had to do was put an imaginary Philippe Petit up in the balcony, gaze up at the stagehand carrying a flashlight, and move their heads in unison as Petit strode, danced, and clowned from one tower to the next. The audience couldn't breathe!

And yes, you *can* set a play in a swimming pool! *Milk and Water*, which takes place during a water aerobics class for nursing mothers, has been buoyantly produced on a bone-dry stage.

So you see where Ionesco's *The Bald Soprano* has taken me—this curious "tragedy of language" that's been running over fifty years at the Théâtre de la Huchette—from exploring the extraordinary ways women communicate to spiraling out into the roar of the universe at large.

A warning should be placed above the marquee: "Caution: This play will change the way you see theatre for the rest of your life."

I'm just one of many who've fallen under its spell.

10

DAVID HENRY HWANG

DAVID HENRY HWANG's plays include *M. Butterfly* (1988 Tony Award, 1989 Pulitzer Prize finalist), *Golden Child* (1997 Obie Award, 1998 Tony Nomination), *Yellow Face* (2008 Obie Award, 2008 Pulitzer Prize finalist), *FOB* (1981 Obie Award), *The Dance and the Railroad* (1982 Drama Desk nomination), *Family Devotion* (1982 Drama Desk Nomination), and *Bondage*. He wrote the libretti for the Broadway musical *Aida*, by Elton John and Tim Rice (coauthor), the revival of Rodgers and Hammerstein's *Flower Drum Song* (2002 Tony nomination), and Disney's *Tarzan*. In opera, his libretti include Philip Glass' *The Voyage* (Metropolitan Opera), Osvaldo Golijov's *Ainadamar* (two 2007 Grammy Awards), Unsuk Chin's *Alice in Wonderland* (Opernwelt 2007 World Premiere of the Year), and Howard Shore's *The Fly*. Hwang also penned the feature films *M. Butterfly*, *Golden Gate*, and *Possession* (coauthor). He serves on the Council of the Dramatists Guild and was appointed by President Clinton to the President's Committee on the Arts and the Humanities. He joined the board of directors of the American Theatre Wing in 2009.

Two Plays, Two Lives

Marsha Norman says every dramatist has a play that got them hooked on the theatre. "The play that changed my life." That play would have been a cathartic experience, propelling me toward becoming who I am today. But, er, who am I?

Asian American Version

My father liked to boast that he could never hold on to a job. When he first came to America from Shanghai in 1950, Henry Hwang ended up at Linfield

College in McMinville, Oregon, where he lived the American Dream of a rich man's son: skipping classes, tooling around in an American convertible, and dating a blonde coed, all while speaking barely a word of English. A year later, Ti-Ti (my paternal grandfather) got caught up in a business scandal in Taiwan, lost all his money, and went to jail. Despite being suddenly reduced to a poor Chinese immigrant, Dad continued to bridle under authority, refusing to take orders from anyone.

Moving to Los Angeles in search of work, he was first hired by a young Chinese American businessman named Edmund Kwoh. Needless to say, Dad was, in due course, fired from that job as well. Still, he remained friends with Edmund, who went on to marry Beulah Quo, an Emmy-nominated actress whom you may remember as one of the gardeners in Polanski's classic movie *Chinatown* ("Bad for the glass"). In 1965 Beulah, along with six other Asian American actors hungry to grow beyond stereotypical Hollywood roles, founded East-West Players, the nation's first Asian American theatre company. By then running his own CPA firm, Dad was persuaded by Beulah to become the fledgling troupe's bookkeeper. In 1968 East-West decided to produce Gian Carlo Menotti's opera *The Medium*. This would be their first musical production, and they needed a piano accompanist.

Enter my mother. Dorothy Huang (not a typo, my mother's maiden name was the same as my father's surname, only with a different English transliteration) had been born into a wealthy Chinese merchant clan based in the Philippines. During World War II she studied piano under the legendary music educator Herbert Zipper, a Viennese Jew who had been released from the Nazi death camp at Buchenwald and traveled to Manila, only to see it occupied by the Japanese. Dr. Zipper recognized Mom's talent and, after the war, suggested her parents send her to college in either America or Switzerland. America being warmer, my mother ended up in 1953 at USC, where she met my father some three weeks after her arrival in Los Angeles. Fifteen years later, the irrepressible Beulah persuaded my mother to serve as pianist for *The Medium*.

My younger sisters, Mimi and Grace, five and four years old, got parked during rehearsals at the home of my Maternal Grandfather's Number One Sister, whose husband was the pastor of a small Chinese American church that met in their home. As a ten-year-old, I was given the option of going to rehearsals, which I usually chose to attend—for a change of scenery, if for no other reason. The troupe worked in the basement of Bethany Presbyterian Church, where Beulah was a member, in the Silver Lake district of Los Angeles.

Rehearsals were held at nights, the basement was dark, and everyone was singing about ghosts. As a child trying to stay out of trouble, I often found myself in shadowy corners, which were even darker than the rest of the room. So I was frightened a good deal of the time, except when I managed to ignore the onstage goings-on, at which point I grew bored. All things being equal, I concluded that it was better to remain scared. The story, which Menotti originally set in Budapest, was moved for this production to post–World War II Japan: a drunken con artist who calls herself Madame Flora performs fake séances for parents grieving for their departed children. Frequently drunk, she abuses both her own daughter and a mute servant boy she has picked up on the streets until she is visited by a—possibly—very real spirit.

I've not heard the operetta since, but, to my child's ear, Menotti's music seemed loud, dissonant, and frequently chaotic: I heard shrieks of terror as Madame Flora's rants grew more disturbed and out of control, her sanity deteriorating. This was not exactly my idea of a good time, but it was fascinating too. As we drew closer to opening night, I grew so familiar with the music that I could follow most of the lines; I still didn't know if I liked the story, but I knew it by heart. With the addition of costumes and makeup, what had once had felt like a cold and distant exercise—grown-ups gathering in a basement to pretend they were characters who sang rather than spoke—became startlingly real.

I was glad when the production ended and I could again spend my nights at home instead of in a church basement watching an old woman sing about losing her marbles. My mother never again assumed accompanist duties for any production more elaborate than a school talent show. Our family never went to the theatre, and I didn't see another musical show until high school.

Looking back, though, I can't help but suspect that those few weeks in the basement of Bethany Presbyterian Church planted seeds in my ten-year-old consciousness that would eventually determine much of my adult life. There I watched people with Asian faces working as actors in a time when such an idea was almost inconceivable in America. Living through a production process, I saw concepts and stories travel from page to stage and, in so doing, bring an entire physical world to life before my eyes. My first theatrical exposure was to opera, which showed the stage to be inherently different than the naturalistic television shows I watched at home; theatre could include movement and music—even people who sang rather than spoke. Present at the infancy of a new troupe, I learned that theatre could be performed not just in big fancy halls, but anywhere you could find a room.

Years later, as a college student, I developed an inexplicable urge to try my hand at writing plays. For my senior year, I wrote one called *FOB*. An acronym for "Fresh Off the Boat," it was a show for Asian actors about conflicts between foreign- and U.S.-born Chinese Americans. Less than two years later, Joe Papp produced *FOB* Off-Broadway at The Public Theater, turning me into a professional playwright. I had already staged the first production myself, however—not in a church basement, but in the lobby of my dormitory.

Professional Playwright Version

I added my name to the sign-up sheet in the lobby of my dormitory at Stanford. This was an opportunity for freshmen to go to "The City" (San Francisco) and see a play at . . . well, at one of the big fancy theatres up there. I had seen exactly one fully produced nonmusical play in my life: when I was a senior in high school, my English teacher, Suzi Dietz (who would go on to a major producing career in California and on Broadway), had directed Arthur Kopit's *Indians*. That show had knocked me out with the size of its vision—its ability to infuse history with the ghosts of the present—as well as its exuberant theatricality. Plays did not have to be like the naturalistic representations I saw on TV; they could include movement and music—even a Wild West show.

Settling down into our seats at San Francisco's American Conservatory Theater, I wondered how my first professional play would stack up against the experimental flourishes of *Indians*. The lights went up to reveal a half circle of men wearing identical structures on their shoulders: metal frames encompassed the actors' heads, leaving their facial features visible, suggesting both animal heads and cages. Their footwear was similarly designed: dark metal frames that gave the actors height and were also vaguely frightening, like some medieval restraining device. As they began to move like horses, a human character traveled to the middle of the stage and began speaking to us about a horse called Nugget. The opening moments of *Equus* evoked religion, mystery, and ritual, sensations I knew in my bones—from church.

I grew up in an extended family of evangelical Christians; at the time, they considered themselves "fundamentalists," though they would start shying away from that term years later, after the events of 9/11. In 1965 my granduncle began organizing a small worship service that met in the living room of his Los Angeles home. We attended services there, and I was baptized in that living room at the age of ten; one could even consider it something of a family church. A few years later, my uncle Eddie (not the founder's son, but a different uncle) took over as pastor, and the growing congregation purchased a church building in the Silver Lake district. This ministry would continue to expand; today it encompasses an association of six member churches throughout southern California.

Uncle Eddie, though warm and relatively open-minded in private, was an old-fashioned fire-and-brimstone preacher in the pulpit. As a child, I would often attend church-related activities three times a week—Sundays, Saturdays for choir practice, and a weekday evening for Bible study. Moreover, extended family gatherings inevitably included conversations about religion and church business.

As the story of *Equus* began to unfold that evening in San Francisco, it spoke to the Christian influences with which I'd been raised. Dr. Martin Dysart, a troubled psychiatrist, recounted a case that had deeply disturbed him: a boy named Alan Strang had been committed to his care after having blinded a stable full of horses. The playwright Peter Shaffer structures *Equus* brilliantly as a psychological and spiritual detective story, with Dysart speaking directly to the audience, then stepping into flashback scenes dramatizing his interactions with Strang and other characters. I saw how the boy was raised by a moralistic but atheistic father and a mother who surreptitiously encouraged their son's fascination with Christian texts and iconography. Eventually Strang developed a fetishistic attachment to horses, which he began to conflate with the forbidden Christian images, particularly those steeped in blood and violence, and eventually constructed his own personal religion with a god he named Equus.

Naturally, Christian imagery, psychology, and sexual repression combined for me into a very potent stew. Though I had always played the role of contrarian in my extended family—pointing out inconsistencies in our faith and shying away from proselytizing duties—I had always considered myself a committed Christian through high school. Now, as a freshman in college, I was living away from my family for the first time and, despite having dutifully attended Bible studies in my dormitory, doubts about my faith had grown more pronounced over the passing months. *Equus* does not set out to debunk religious faith—on the contrary, it questions the rationalism of contemporary society, as embodied in the role of the humanistic priests known as psychiatrists, and our dismissal of religious ecstasy. Nevertheless, Shaffer's confrontation of my core issues, the verve with which he posed his questions, and his imaginative variations on biblical stories and texts—these excited my imagination, my emotions, and perhaps even my soul. Such themes collided and recombined with growing intensity as the story marched on, leading to the climactic scene where Strang recreates his blinding of the horses. Not

Michael Keys-Hall (top) and Daniel Zippi in the 1976 American Conservatory The-atre production of Peter Shaffer's Equus *at the Geary Theater in San Francisco. (Photo reprinted with permission of the estate of William Ganslen, courtesy of the John Willis Theatre World/Screen World Archive)*

incidentally, that moment also included the first full-frontal nudity I'd ever seen onstage. In the play's final image of spiritual agony and confusion, Dysart seemed to mirror the jumble of emotions and sensations whirling within me. I left my seat excited and emotionally spent, amazed by the theatre's power to call up the very ecstasy for which the psychiatrist yearned in his own life—an ecstasy I had not felt in my years of churchgoing.

Over the following years, *Equus* continued to transform my life in new and surprising ways. When I began writing *M. Butterfly*, the play for which I remain best known, I consciously chose to steal Shaffer's structure, one he returned to for his masterful *Amadeus*. As in those plays, *M. Butterfly* also begins with the lead character in a state of turmoil, one who tells his story to the audience as he plays himself in flashback scenes.

When Stuart Ostrow decided to produce *M. Butterfly* on Broadway in 1988, he had only one idea for a director: John Dexter, who had staged the original production of *Equus* in London and on Broadway. Though the version I saw in San Francisco was not directed by Dexter, almost all productions in those early years following the show's initial Broadway run (and many to this day) incorporated the iconography created by Shaffer, Dexter, and the designer John Napier: fetishistic horse costumes, a ritualistic amphitheatre-like set, and a movement vocabulary influenced by traditional Asian theatre. Needless to say, I jumped at the possibility of working with the director whose role in the birth of *Equus* had been so critical that no one who saw the play could forget that first, iconic production.

Dexter came to *M. Butterfly* with a reputation for difficult and demanding behavior, sometimes to the point of cruelty. He passed away in 1990, just a few short years after *M. Butterfly* opened on Broadway, and the title of his posthumously published autobiography acknowledged that image: *The Honourable Beast*. In his dealings with me, however, Dexter was always kind, polite, and respectful. I did several drafts of the play before we went into rehearsal and at one point inserted a new scene which included full-frontal male nudity. When Dexter read the rewrite, he smiled. "Well, I've been here before, of course. It's very important how we stage the nudity, I learned that on 'Equus.'" To illustrate, he extended his fingers to imitate a penis and hung them alongside his face: "If you have a penis here and the Lunts here," indicating his own face, "everyone's looking at the penis."

The nudity survived as part of the climactic scene of my finished script. About a year after *M. Butterfly* opened, I had the pleasure of meeting Peter Shaffer. "Thank you," I gushed nervously. "I got the structure for *M. Butterfly* from you." Though he might have berated me for my theft, Shaffer's response could not have been more gracious: he thanked me for the compliment. Today, some twenty years after my play's Broadway opening, it now shares one more similarity with *Equus*: no one who ever saw the show can forget that original production.

Watching *Equus* again, in its 2008 Broadway revival starring Richard Griffiths and Daniel Radcliffe, I was struck by how many lines I remembered, how many structural similarities it shared with *M. Butterfly*. Alan Strang's religious world includes a genealogy: "Prince begat Prance, . . ." and so on, leading to the birth of *Equus*. In the genealogy of my life as a playwright, however, *Equus* begat *M. Butterfly*.

It seems to me that, over the course of our time here, we live several different lives—sometimes simultaneously. The wonder of theatre is that any production, in any space, experienced at any age, can change any of those lives.

11

DAVID IVES

© 2009 Susan Johann

DAVID IVES had his first professional production at twenty-one. A graduate of Northwestern University and the Yale School of Drama and a former Guggenheim Fellow in playwriting, he has written over thirty one-act plays and is probably best known for his evenings of one-acts, *All in the Timing* and *Time Flies*. His full-length plays include *New Jerusalem: The Interrogation of Baruch de Spinoza*, *Venus in Fur*, *Polish Joke*, and *Is He Dead?* (adapted from Mark Twain). He has translated Feydeau's *A Flea in Her Ear*, Yasmina Reza's *A Spanish Play*, and Corneille's *The Liar*. He also co-wrote the book for *Irving Berlin's White Christmas*, has adapted over twenty-five musicals for New York City's Encores series, and is the author of three young-adult novels: *Monsieur Eek*, *Scrib*, and *Voss, or: How I Come to America and Am Hero, Mostly*. He lives in New York with his wife, Martha.

Indelicately Unbalanced

I grew up in Polish Catholic, blue-collar South Chicago in the 1950s and 1960s, and theatre was not exactly a favored local sport around the neighborhood. Making homemade kielbasa at Easter? Yes. Bowling? Definitely. Shakespeare? No.

Still, my parents for some reason were interested enough in the theatre to go to a play every now and again, and sometimes disappeared to some mysterious entity called a "dinner theatre." I recall them heading into the Loop one evening tricked out in Saturday-night finery to take in something called *A Man for All Seasons*, a show that excited my interest because the cast included Albert Dekker, whom I knew from playing the evil Dr. Cyclops in the movie of the same name. (This was the same manly, baritone Albert Dekker who was some years later found dead in women's clothing, having hanged himself in his home, whether by accident or intent we will never know.) My parents also occasionally treated us three kids during Christmas season to a road show passing through town. My father went with me to see a *Witness for the Prosecution* wannabe called *Hostile Witness* with Ray Milland the same Saturday afternoon my mother took my sisters to see *Half a Sixpence* with Tommy Steele further down State Street. I'm sure my father went because of Ray Milland, not because of any play. My father spent my childhood sitting in his armchair puffing on Pall Malls and reciting to me the bit players and supporting actors of old movies as they ghosted across our tiny black-and-white television screen. "That's Eduardo Ciannelli. . . That's Albert Dekker . . . That's Hume Cronyn. . . ."

Of course, theatre was far more present and accounted for in the general culture at the time. Ed Sullivan showed scenes from current Broadway plays on his immensely popular Sunday-evening variety show on CBS. Those were the days when men went to the theatre in jackets and ties, not flip-flops, T-shirts, and shorts, nor would anyone think of sucking on a plastic water bottle during *Death of a Salesman*. Those were also the days when Caedmon Records brought out major contemporary plays on multi-record sets of vinyl, and the public service radio station in Chicago broadcast them. I remember listening raptly to *Incident at Vichy* while trying to do my high school homework at our kitchen table. I recall being particularly riveted by a character who kept complaining that the fascist officials had *measured his nose*. The specificity and pungency of that detail caught my ear and gave me then a little inward shiver, maybe because I was conscious my own nose was growing to outrageous proportions. My mother once, for reasons I don't recall—maybe a birthday around the time I was twelve or so—gave me a special treat, taking me to see John Gavin (or was it John Saxon?) in *Ten Little Indians* (or was it *The Mousetrap*?) at the Drury Lane Theatre in Evergreen Park (now gone). This was not a treat for theatrical reasons. At that age, I was not addicted to the theatre. I was addicted to Agatha Christie.

I say I was not addicted to theatre, yet it was around that time that I wrote my first play: an adaptation of a pulp crime novel from the 1930s called *Mr. Strang*. ("The punch packing story of a mysterious individual who sets out singlehandedly to break up the racket of Parole!" says the flap on the foxed and yellowed copy I have before me.) I planned to present—that is, produce and perform—my adaptation of *Mr. Strang* for my Boy Scout troop at our monthly meeting. I figured I would build the set myself, wrangle the costumes, write the script, and, of course, play the lead, the inscrutable figure of Strang, a suave tough who had a butler named Maxie and seemed able to appear and disappear from crime scenes at will, a talent I personally aspired to. Why not? Almost all my role models at the time wore tights, capes, and hoods. With a little luck and determination, maybe I too could spend my life singlehandedly breaking up the racket of Parole. Little did I know my life would be spent *entre paroles*, not Parole.

I cast some of my friends in the supporting parts, I started cobbling a set together in our basement from odds and ends of lumber, and sat down at the dining room table to translate this gory, violent three-hundred-page thriller into scenes with dialogue. In the event, there were three major problems with my plan, never mind wrangling costumes. First, I had no idea it was so hard to turn three hundred pages of gory, violent novel into theatrical dialogue. I ended up with probably ten small notebook pages of handwritten exchanges and convinced myself that that was probably just about right for length. (My first short play, inadvertently.) Second, I had and still have no talent whatsoever with my hands, so that the "set" ended up being a few bent threepenny nails hanging out of some stained two-by-fours, none of which fitted together. Third, I was missing a crucial piece of theatrical information: I did not know that every member of the cast had to have a copy of the script. I learned my lines, I passed the script on to the next guy to learn his, and he lost the script. My scoutmaster, Mr. Lewandowski, was not pleased when the promised production did not appear on the scheduled night. It probably meant he had to haul out some old Indian lore or show us how to tie more knots or something. What I still don't understand is how I got from this novel that I found stuck in one of our bookshelves to the idea of turning it into a play.

The first show I'd ever seen was around the age of seven, a production of *Pinocchio* that my mother took us kids to one afternoon at the old Goodman Theatre, back then a musty, fusty, rather funereal joint with lighting to match. All the characters in the show were played by actors except Pinocchio, who was a marionette in a puppeteer's booth at center stage. Even then I thought that was pretty interesting—this other smaller world sitting there in the middle of a larger empty space. A stage within a stage. A mixing of different kinds of realities. After the play I stood in the lobby with my program and got the autographs of the Fox and the Blue Fairy. (Who was that young actress in the blue tulle and the satin heels and the wings? What were her aspirations, what was her biography, and where is she now?)

I continued to go to the theatre in high school, particularly toward the latter end of high school, which in my case was a Catholic seminary established to prepare young men for the priesthood. This school had a theatrical tradition I've never heard of in any other school anywhere, and which I highly recommend to all institutions of secondary education: every year in May the senior class put on a show called the Senior Mock in which they sent up the faculty.

The show was written, produced, and acted by the seniors, and though the school's rector had to vet the script beforehand, he never censored anything but obscenities. Anything else was fair game: Mr. Peters' Elmer Fudd–like speech impediment, Father Curran's lubricious leer when strolling through the locker room, Mr. Hild's barking voice and smoking habit in English class. I knew the latter very well because in our year's Senior Mock I played Harry Hild, complete with cigarette in mouth while coaching the track team, in a section that I improvised, along with a song I performed *a capella* mocking Father Spizziri's hippie-dippie religiosity. The whole school came to watch the show, packing the auditorium—the faculty too, since it was considered very bad form for the faculty not to be present to take their punishment. I well remember Mr. Hild complimenting me on my performance the day after the show—as he puffed on a cigarette in the school corridor. The Quigley Preparatory Seminary's Senior Mock was a tribute to popular theatre, and, though I didn't know it, we were doing the same thing Aristophanes did in Athens in 400 B.C.: satirizing the people we knew, thinking about our lives by acting them out, and acting out. What an extraordinary introduction to the power of theatre, and how brave of that school (now gone) to allow such a thing. In certain ways, that show was the most important play of my life because it made theatre personal, immediate, meaningful, and fun.

That same final year in high school I wrote a full-length play called *The Quiet Seasons* (title taken from T. S. Eliot, of course) about (what else?) a young seminarian torn between the Church and a Girl. Probably a seminarian with a nose of extraordinary proportions. I can't say. The script is mercifully lost.

Someone in the 1960s—maybe it was Eva Le Gallienne—made one of our country's regular and unsuccessful attempts at establishing a national repertory theatre. The company toured some shows around the country, including a production of Molière's *The Imaginary Invalid*. A number of my fellow seminarians decided to attend this cultural event en masse, and we bought a bloc of tickets. Most memorably, one of my classmates warned me that if I wore white socks and black shoes to the show the rest of our theatre party would have nothing to do with me. It may have been the last time I ever wore white socks with black shoes, but I doubt it. I think everybody should wear white socks with black shoes all the time. Fred Astaire wore them in movies. Anyway, the Molière production had a fabulously funny maid with a clever, pert, bouncing walk. That maid was played by the actress Sloane Shelton, whom years later, when I came to New York, I would get to know on a waving, hello-how-are-you basis. How odd. Forty years later I still see her in her tutu-like skirt and flat black shoes bouncing across the stage with something—a tray?—in her hand. I too wore black shoes that night, sans white socks. Decades later I was given to understand that the sassy fellow seminarian with strong feelings about white socks had taken to picking up rough trade and getting himself beaten up for sex. In context, white socks seem pretty harmless. I wonder if he's still alive.

Then came an afternoon during my senior year when I went to the Studebaker Theatre (gone now) to see a matinee of Edward Albee's *A Delicate Balance* with Hume Cronyn and Jessica Tandy. I certainly knew who Edward Albee was, as I had spent the previous summer sitting on our porch reading *Who's Afraid of Virginia Woolf?* over and over, half aloud, intoxicated by the rhythm of the lines and tickled by the bite of the invective. In fact, Albee had recently come to Chicago to speak to a hallful of blue-haired ladies at the Conrad Hilton, and I'd bought a ticket and gone to hear him. He was an astonishing thing to a seventeen-year-old kid: *a living, talking playwright, in the flesh.* Also a wildly famous if not notorious one, in the wake of *Virginia Woolf*'s success and reputation as unspeakable filth. After his lecture excoriating critics and popular tastes in plays, a lady rose to ask a question.

"Mr. Albee," she said, "you keep using the phrase *an educated taste*. What do you mean by *an educated taste*?"

"What I mean by *an educated taste*," Edward Albee said fluidly, "is someone who has the same tastes that I have."

How. Cool.

After the lecture I happened to notice, through an open doorway, Mr. Albee standing in a sort of carpeted gallery outside the lecture hall. I approached timidly as he ordered a vodka tonic from someone, at which point I decided I would always drink vodka tonics, and order them with the same suave elegance. He turned to me with that ferocious (it's still ferocious today) look of his. There he was. A great playwright. *And yet he was very, very nice.* I recall being bold enough to venture the opinion that Eugene O'Neill's dialogue seemed kind of clumsy. *And Edward Albee agreed with me.* He spoke casually about it, with a shrug, as if it weren't sacrilege to say such a thing about a Great American Playwright. I have no doubt I walked back out onto Michigan Avenue encased in a golden aura. I'd had my first professional theatrical conversation—and it had been the equivalent of a kid collaring Euripides just outside the Theatre of Dionysus and dissing Aeschylus with him.

And so, by forthrights and meanders, I ended up in the balcony of the

Studebaker Theatre one Saturday afternoon watching *A Delicate Balance*. I may as well have been in the front car of the Cyclone at Coney Island, just cresting the top of that first high, steep hill and starting the plunge. There are so few moments in life about which one can say: *Everything was entirely different after that*. The two hours of that play, passing in an ecstatic flash, were such a moment. I had never seen anything like that show, had never seen people tear themselves apart so, or need each other so, had never heard such eloquence or such honesty, had never seen human beings make themselves, through speech and gesture, so transparent they may as well have been behind a fluoroscopic screen. Hume Cronyn performing the speech about the cat ("The cat that I had . . . when I was—well, a year or so before I *met* you . . .") has to be one of the great moments of my life, and I knew it as I was hearing it. The balcony itself in my recollection feels as if it's tipping forward to spill me out onto the stage, I'm so dizzy, so undone, so high.

My life as I had known it was over.

After the performance I stood waiting outside the theatre and sure enough, down an alleyway from the stage door came Jessica Tandy, headed for a waiting taxi, followed by Hume Cronyn. I stopped them and got their autographs on my program and stammered something to Mr. Cronyn about how much I had loved the show. And then they got in the cab and drove away.

I still have that signed program and the ticket stub to that matinee. Price: $3.65. The fact that I kept them both means that I knew something very important already. The fact is, I may as well have gone home that afternoon and put a note on the kitchen table: *Dear Mom and Dad. I am going to be a playwright. Don't try to stop me*. The decision was taken. It was all over. I wanted to spend my lifetime chasing what I'd seen and heard in that vertiginous balcony that day.

Flash forward twenty years. Suitcase in hand, I am riding up the elevator of the Mondrian Hotel on the Sunset Strip. It's a balmy Sunday evening in spring in the late 1980s. I have come to Los Angeles for my first Hollywood meeting. The following afternoon at three o'clock I'm supposed to meet with the head of Universal Studios and pitch an idea for a screenplay. If he likes the idea, I'll get a job writing the script.

The elevator doors open on the fourth floor to let me out, and there, standing before me in a paisley silk dressing gown, an ascot, and slippers, is Hume Cronyn, looking right and left rather distractedly. I step out of the elevator. He continues to look about. I cannot help myself.

"Hello, Mr. Cronyn," I say.

Jessica Tandy as Agnes and Hume Cronyn as Tobias in the 1966 Broadway production of Edward Albee's A Delicate Balance *at the Martin Beck Theatre. (Alix Jeffry photograph, copyright © The Harvard Theatre Collection, Houghton Library, courtesy of the John Willis Theatre World/Screen World Archive)*

He turns to me. "Oh. Hello. Have you seen the maid?" That familiar nasal, honking voice. The voice that had once told me about a cat. . . .

"I haven't seen the maid," I said. "I've just arrived. . . ."

We start down the corridor together, inadvertently side by side. Once again I cannot help myself.

"Mr. Cronyn," I venture, "I have to tell you . . . you changed my life. You and your wife."

"Really?" he says, stopping in his tracks. "How is that?"

I tell him about seeing *A Delicate Balance* twenty years before. He hears me out, clearly pleased, his hands jammed in the pockets of his dressing gown *just the way people do it onstage.*

He says to me, "What are you doing in Hollywood?"

"I've come for my first—possible—Hollywood job. Tomorrow."

"Where?"

"Universal."

"Jessie and I are filming at Universal. Why don't I take you to lunch in the commissary?"

"Um," I say. "All right."

We shake hands and go our separate ways, parting at the intersection of two corridors. I find my hotel room, turn on the light, and stand there unbelieving. *I've just met Hume Cronyn.* I think to myself, Well, that was amazing, but that was that. I have an impulse to call my father and tell him I just met Hume Cronyn, but my father has been dead now for several years. . . .

My phone rings. How can this be? I don't know anyone in Hollywood. I pick up.

"Yes?"

"Hello," I hear from the other end, "is this David?"

"Yes . . ."

"This is Hume. Come to soundstage 22 around one o'clock and tell them I'm expecting you."

"All right," I say as if this is the most normal thing in the world. "I'll see you then."

"See you then."

And so the next day I drive my rental car in the gate of Universal Studios, park it, and walk to soundstage 22, where a smiling young lady with a clipboard is standing like a blue-jeaned California angel at a gate, waiting for me in a set of studio headphones.

I say (tossing it off, casually): "Hume Cronyn is expecting me."

"Oh, yes, David," she says. "He said you should meet him in his trailer. I'll take you there."

A real Hollywood trailer. As we approach I see, through the screen door, *Hume*, standing up to greet me, tossing aside a Robertson Davies novel.

"Come on in," he says. "Take a seat and tell me about yourself. Jessie ought to be here in a second. She'd come to lunch with us but she has to go back and film."

So I sit down and tell *Hume Cronyn* about myself. Then I hear the door and instinctively rise. Jessica Tandy is walking in. She is the most striking woman I've ever seen. Luminous, with swept-back white hair and porcelain skin and blue eyes like cut glass. The original Blanche Dubois. The woman who was lifted up onstage by Marlon Brando ("We've had this date with each other from the beginning!") every night for two years in one of the greatest of American plays.

"So," says Jessica Tandy to me, not able to suppress her smile, "you're the young man whose life we changed. Tell me about it."

And so I did. And they were both *very, very nice*.

And Hume did take me to lunch at the commissary.

And I did indeed pitch my idea to the head of Universal that afternoon.

And I got the job.

And as I drove out of the studio gate that pellucid afternoon, I felt as if nothing bad could ever, ever happen to me. And if it did, it wouldn't matter very much.

12

DONALD MARGULIES

DONALD MARGULIES' plays include *Brooklyn Boy*, *Dinner with Friends*, *Sight Unseen*, *Collected Stories*, *The Loman Family Picnic*, *God of Vengeance*, *What's Wrong with This Picture?*, *The Model Apartment*, *Shipwrecked! An Entertainment—The Amazing Adventures of Louis de Rougemont (as told by himself)*, and *Time Stands Still*. He has won a Lucille Lortel Award, an American Theatre Critics Award, two Los Angeles Drama Critics Circle Awards, two Obie Awards, two Dramatists Guild Hull-Warriner Awards, five Drama Desk Award nominations, two Pulitzer Prize nominations, and one Pulitzer Prize. His works have been performed at major theatres across the United States and around the world. Mr. Margulies has received grants from the National Endowment for the Arts, the New York Foundation for the Arts, and the John Simon Guggenheim Memorial Foundation. He was the recipient of the 2000 Sidney Kingsley Award for Outstanding Achievement in the Theatre, and in 2005 he was honored by the American Academy of Arts and Letters with an Award in Literature. Mr. Margulies is an alumnus of New Dramatists and serves on the council of the Dramatists Guild of America. He is an adjunct professor of English and theatre studies at Yale University.

A Playwright's Search for the Spiritual Father

Sometime in the early '60s, when I was around nine years old, my parents told me and my older brother that instead of spending my father's one-week summer vacation on a bus tour of the Berkshires or Pennsylvania Dutch country (as we had done before), this time we would be spending it in *The City*. To Brooklynites like us, *The City* meant Manhattan and, until my parents announced our vacation plans, I thought of it as a special place that existed solely for school trips to the Planetarium or the occasional family outing to Radio City.

"What are we gonna do in *The City*?" I asked. It was not, as far as I could tell, a place where people from Brooklyn spent the night, let alone a whole week.

"We're gonna see shows!" my parents told me, which meant, of course, Broadway. (We were cultural Jews; the only fervor that existed in our household wasn't centered on religion but on show business.)

So my mother and father and brother and I put on our nice clothes and, suitcases in tow, got on the Brighton local (we didn't own a car) and took the hour-long ride from Sheepshead Bay to Rockefeller Center. We checked into a cheap hotel in the West Fifties and for the next six days saw every hit in town, shows like *Funny Girl, Fiddler on the Roof, Hello, Dolly!* As the house lights dimmed each night, plus matinees on Wednesday, Saturday, and Sunday, I remember feeling almost unbearably excited by what lay ahead.

When I recently recalled my family's theatregoing vacations, they took me on the mythic proportions of something we used to do all the time— until I realized that we probably did it only twice. Those two weeks, spent during two different theatrical seasons in the same funky midtown hotel, have blurred in my memory but their impact was powerful.

Herb Gardner's *A Thousand Clowns* was the first nonmusical play I ever saw, and I remember how the muscles in my face hurt from grinning in pleasure for two hours. I felt privileged being in a grand Broadway theatre packed with well-dressed adults and being let in on jokes they so obviously enjoyed; I was thrilled to add my small sound to all that laughter. For a boy like me, whose father worked all the time, it must have been invigorating to see a play about a man who preferred being home to toiling at a demoralizing job. In retrospect, it seems fitting that my first exposure to drama was a play about a complex father figure and his surrogate son, for the theme of fathers and sons has long figured in my plans and in my life.

The central character of my first full-length play, *Pals* (1979), had a lot in common with my father; I see now that I was trying to concretize my father's speech and thought processes as a way of understanding him. The grief-stricken father in *What's Wrong With This Picture?* was a further exploration of my own father, but it wasn't until after his death in 1987 (my mother had died nine years earlier) that I was able to truly uncover him.

My black comedy, *The Loman Family Picnic* (1989), is about a middle-class Jewish family in extremis over the oldest son's bar mitzvah. The cultural, economic, and social pretensions surrounding that event lead to the beleaguered father's terrifying explosion. Giving voice to that inarticulate rage helped me find my father.

In my 1991 play, *Sight Unseen*, the father is offstage, a shadowy figure whose recent death jolts the protagonist, the painter Jonathan Waxman, into examining his loss of cultural identity and artistic purpose. His journey leads him to Patricia, the woman with whom he long ago had a relationship, which symbolized the themes of his life and which remains unresolved. "I'm nobody's son anymore, Patty," he tells her. "They're all gone now, all the disappointable people."

My parents, Charlene and Bob Margulies, were of the generation of lower-middle-class Jews who were raised during the Depression and came of age during World War II. Like many married couples of that generation, my mother was the *balebusteh*, the powerhouse who embodied the cockeyed optimism and practicality of that time, while my father was the eternally haunted one who lived in fear of losing his job (even though he worked for the same people for forty years) and who was disturbed by change of any kind.

My father was a taciturn man, physically affectionate but prone to mysterious silences, who worked six, sometimes seven, days a week selling wallpaper in a store on Flatbush Avenue. His days routinely began at six in the morning and didn't end until eleven at night, but his rare days off were often devoted to playing records on the living room hi-fi. The great composers whose music wafted through our tiny apartment weren't Beethoven and Mozart but Loesser and Styne and Rodgers and Hammerstein. That was my father at his most content; playing his Broadway musical cast albums, dozens of them, on Sunday mornings throughout my childhood. I was the only kid in the sixth grade who knew by heart the entire score of *Happy Hunting*, an obscure Ethel Merman musical I heard countless times.

When I was small, my father and I would watch old movies on television together, the beloved movies of his youth, and he'd grill me on the character actors. "Donnie, who's that?" he'd ask, pointing to the wizened old woman on the TV screen. "Maria Ouspenskaya," I'd tell him, having learned my lessons well. But as my brother and I grew more intellectually and creatively curious, he began to distance himself. We were, no doubt, challenging sons for a stolid, unanalytical father; he responded by abdicating, by leaving our education entirely up to my mother. We were fortunate that she loved to read and instilled that love of books in her children.

As a youngster, I was troubled that my father showed no interest in reading anything but the *Daily News*. How could someone not read books?

Jason Robards Jr. as Murray and Sandy Dennis as Sandra in the 1962 Broadway pro-
duction of Herb Gardner's A Thousand Clowns. *(Photo by Shel Secunda, courtesy of*
the John Willis Theatre World/Screen World Archive)

I took it as a personal affront, a form of rejection. Unconsciously, I began to search for spiritual fathers, creative men with whom I could commune intellectually, older men who could make me make sense of the world. My father's silence created in me a hunger for words that drew me to surrogate fathers, men I knew only through what they wrote. Herb Gardner may have been my earliest spiritual father, but Arthur Miller came into my life not long after.

I was eleven years old when I read *Death of a Salesman*, and I remember the guilt and shame I felt for recognizing in the Lomans truths about my own family: that my mother shared Linda's chauvinism and, most frightening of all, that my father, then barely forty, might turn out to be a Willy himself. But the play's uncanny reflection of my life and worst fears also exhilarated me and made me feel less alone. I studied it with great fascination, as if it were a key to understanding what was happening to the people I loved, so that I might somehow alter my family's fate. As a boy growing up in Trump Village (the Coney Island housing project built by Donald Trump's father), I imagined that our high-rise was one of the buildings that overshadowed the Lomans' modest house. Years later, in *The Loman Family Picnic*, I took that notion and made a play out of it.

After Miller, and as adolescence approached, I discovered in J. D. Salinger a spiritual father so empathic that he seemed to know how I felt about everything. Once I'd read *The Catcher in the Rye*, I devoured all of Salinger (just three slim paperbacks) and made a mission of tracking down the uncollected stories in old volumes of *The New Yorker*. I wanted more, but Salinger, who still writes but refuses to publish, proved to be the ultimate withholding father.

Philip Roth was not withholding. He was brainy, naughty, and bursting with words: the cool daddy with whom one could talk about sex. I was fifteen when I first read *Portnoy's Complaint* and for all the wrong reasons; I was scanning for tales of sexy shiksas, but what I found were stunning insights into what it meant to be a Jew and a man. Even though he was nearly a generation older, Roth and I seemed to have grown up together, surrounded by many of the same relatives, sharing many similar experiences. He opened a window for me and let fresh air into a stuffy Brooklyn apartment and gave me (and still gives me) the courage to write what I know.

Because as a child I drew well, I was encouraged by my parents and teachers to pursue the visual arts. Art dominated my public school education and, when it came time to go to college, I was offered a scholarship to Pratt Institute. I lasted at Pratt for a year and a half. I was already itching to write (what, I had no idea), but I found no one there to guide me. I transferred to the State University of New York at Purchase, then the upstart liberal-arts college in the SUNY system, where I made mentors of literate and wise art professors like Abe Ajay and Antonio Frasconi. I found inspiration in Giacometti drawings, Schwitters collages, and Diebenkorn paintings.

I was a disgruntled art major with literary aspirations when I walked into the office of Julius Novick, the theatre critic, who taught dramatic literature at Purchase. I boldly asked if he would be willing to sponsor me in a playwriting tutorial. He said yes and could not have imagined the impact that his decision was to have on my life: I was given permission to write. It was about this time that I discovered *The Homecoming* and *The Sound and the Fury*. On the face of it, Pinter's stark, nightmarish black comedy and Faulkner's gorgeously poetic family saga had little in common and yet, in my mind, they coexisted, thrillingly. If I was to be a writer, why couldn't I be an offspring of *all* these spiritual fathers, a son of Pinter and Faulkner—and Miller and Salinger and Roth and Giacometti and Schwitters?

After I graduated, I supported myself as a graphic designer while I wrote plays. My entry into the real world of New York theatre in the early '80s eventually brought me into contact with the man who was the surrogate father to an entire generation of theatre people: Joseph Papp. Stories of his enormous heart (and his capriciousness) are now legend, and they're all probably true. When Joe loved you, he loved you extravagantly; when he loved you less, you could feel the drop in temperature.

At the peak of his affection, I'd run into him in the lobby of The Public Theater and he'd ask, "How's my Jewish playwright?" and I'd stand there and kibbitz with Joe Papp, as I would with any one of my relatives, and have the exciting feeling that there, in Joe's nurturing hands, under Joe's approving eye, at the age of twenty-nine, I had somehow arrived.

My father lived to see *Found a Peanut*, my Off-Broadway debut, at The Public in 1984. The opening night party was pure Joe Papp: a bar mitzvah boy's dream come true, complete with brisket, potato pancakes, hot dogs, egg creams, and loud rock and roll. I brought my father across the crowded room to introduce him to Joe. There was something exquisite in the meeting of these two men: my father, the working-class lover of theatre, the lifelong fan, meeting the self-made impresario. A crossing of the bridge at last, from Brooklyn to *The City*. Father of my childhood, meet father of my professional life. "Bob Margulies, meet Joe Papp."

"You've got quite a son here," Joe said as he shook my father's hand.

"Thanks to you."

"What do you mean, thanks to *me*," Joe Papp yelled at my father, "thanks to *you!*" as if to say, "*I'm not his father, you are! Take responsibility for what's yours once and for all and be proud!*"

Not until I was an adult did I understand that, in his lonely abdication, my father sought refuge from his demons, from the terrible fear that, not having had a relationship with his own father, he wouldn't know how to be a father himself; rather than try and fail, he simply retreated into silence. Years after I became a playwright, I realized that playwriting—the craft of dramatizing the unspoken—provided me with the tools I needed to get inside my father's head and figure out what he was thinking. Through the echoes of my father that occur in my plays, I have been able to give him a voice he only rarely used in life.

This essay first appeared in the New York Times, June 21, 1992. It is reprinted here with permission of the author.

LYNN NOTTAGE

© 2009 Susan Johann

LYNN NOTTAGE's Pulitzer Prize–winning play *Ruined* played an extended run in 2009 Off-Broadway at Manhattan Theatre Club (coproduction with Goodman Theatre in Chicago). *Ruined* has also received an Obie Award, the Lucille Lortel Award, the New York Drama Critics' Circle Award for Best Play, a Drama Desk Award, and an Outer Critics Circle Award. Other plays include *Intimate Apparel* (New York Drama Critics' Circle Award for Best Play; Roundabout, CENTERSTAGE, South Coast Rep); *Fabulation, or the Re-Education of Undine* (Obie Award; Playwrights Horizons, London's Tricycle Theatre); *Crumbs from the Table of Joy*; *Las Meninas*; *Mud, River, Stone*; *Por'knockers*; and *Poof!*

Nottage is the recipient of numerous awards, including the 2007 MacArthur Fellowship ("genius grant"), the National Black Theatre Festival's August Wilson Playwright Award, the 2004 PEN/Laura Pels Award for Drama, and the 2005 John Simon Guggenheim Memorial Foundation Grant for Playwriting, as well as fellowships from the Lucille Lortel Foundation, Manhattan Theatre Club, New Dramatists, and the New York Foundation for the Arts. Lynn's most recent publications include *Intimate Apparel and Fabulation* (Theatre Communications Group) and an anthology of her plays, *Crumbs from the Table of Joy and Other Plays* (Theatre Communications Group). She is a member of the Dramatists Guild, an alumna of New Dramatists, and a graduate of Brown University and the Yale School of Drama, where she is a visiting lecturer.

Succotash on Ice

Ben Hodges: The title of the book is *The Play That Changed My Life*. Were there influences that you could point to that had a large impact on you?

Lynn Nottage: Well, I guess the best way for me to answer this question is to go back to my very, very first memory of going to the theatre, which was seeing a production of a children's play at a community college in Brooklyn. The show was called *Succotash on Ice*. I mention it because it really must have made a tremendous psychic impression, because after all these years—and I have seen hundreds of plays—I still remember the extraordinary moment when this oversized refrigerator on stage opened up and inside there were talking lima beans and corn, and I was absolutely entranced. And I think that was the first moment that I was seduced by the possibilities of theatre. I remember turning to my mother, with my mouth wide open, speechless—I didn't even have language to ask her what was going or express my wonder. I was just like, "Do you see what I'm seeing? Talking lima beans?" And so, you know, we can speak about plays that stylistically and intellectually influenced us, such as *Mother Courage* and *A Raisin in the Sun*. They are plays that were really very, very important to me when I first encountered them. They challenged me to engage the social and political sides of my brain, but I have to turn to something like *Succotash on Ice* as being the play that really transformed me, because it opened up a whole new creative universe for me. It is where I really feel that I understood how magical and special theatre could be.

Hodges: Were there dramatic influences in your school or were other early influences like that? Did literature or television impact you early on before you began to go see shows regularly?

Nottage: Well, you know it's interesting, because I think I am some sort of anomaly. I began to see theatre from a very young age. I grew up in New York City. One of my earliest and fragmented memories was seeing a production of *Hair* on Broadway, I couldn't have been much more than six years old. I also remember seeing *Purlie,* and I remember seeing *Hello, Dolly!*—the all-black production—with Pearl Bailey descending a flight of steps in full regalia. I grew up going to the theatre. It really was my first form of entertainment. Television didn't come into my life until I was a little older, because we didn't have a television until I was about ten or eleven years old. I think that my creative outlet was going to see plays, which, granted, you could do for considerably less money back then.

Hodges: Why do you think that your parents—if it was your parents who took you to the theatre—

Nottage: It was absolutely my parents that took me to theatre. My parents were civil servants. My mother was a schoolteacher. My father worked as a social worker for the city and the state. But, I think that they had the souls of frustrated artists. They were people who always—from as long as I can

Louis Gossett as George Murchison, Ruby Dee as Ruth Younger, and Sidney Poitier as Walter Lee Younger in the 1959 Broadway production of Lorraine Hansberry's A Raisin in the Sun, *at the Ethel Barrymore Theatre. (Photo courtesy of the John Willis Theatre World/Screen World Archive)*

remember—cultivated friendships with artists, writers and musicians. They most definitely cultivated my interest in the arts. I think that, because they were so passionate about art and saw it as an integral part of our life, by extension I became really interested in the arts. Why? You know, it is probably a question that I should sit down and ask my dad before he goes—where did that passion come from in him? Even when you visit my house today you will see that every single space on the wall is filled with some sort of painting or poster. It is literally cluttered with art, but there is still the impulse to collect more.

Hodges: I think you were very lucky.

Nottage: I was. It's as I get older that I realize how blessed I was to grow up in a house where art was valued as much as all other intellectual pursuits.

Hodges: And it also seems like there was an active effort to expose you particularly at a very early age to theatre. Or was it just that they couldn't get a babysitter?

Nottage: My parents were incredibly interested in the theatre and as a result dragged their children along with them. It was part of their philosophy as parents to include us in their lives, rather than building their lives around us. I think it made for a richer experience. They didn't want to exclude us from their passion. Were their times when I was bored and confused by what I encountered? Yes, but those times were equally balanced by moments of great discovery. There were things that I felt at the time may not have necessarily been appropriate for us to see, but my mom said, "I want to see this, and I don't have a babysitter. You're comin' with me." You know, plays like *Hair*. [*Laughs*.]

Hodges: Did you find yourself gravitating toward the performance aspect as you grew up in school, or was this something that kept you more as a spectator?

Nottage: I was always an incredibly shy child. I liked performing, but I don't feel that I had that gene that a lot of actors and performers have which permits them to go in front of an audience and really enjoy themselves. So whenever I went out in front of an audience I felt incredibly self-conscious and would sweat profusely. It's not that I was a bad performer—I just never fully enjoyed that aspect of making theatre. So I think that from an early age I was interested in being on the other side. When I was young I wrote plays that my brother and I would perform for my family and their friends in our parlor. When I was in high school, I went to the High School of Music and Art; I studied music and I always wrote music to be performed by others, but

I rarely performed it myself. I just was never interested in being a performer, but I was always interested in shaping the theatrical experience.

Hodges: This is interesting because I think you are the person in this book who may have seen more productions by the time they got to high school than anybody else.

Nottage: You know what, I think I could give most people a run for their money. I really do feel like I indirectly grew up in the theatre. I was an active engaged theatregoer, which in many ways shaped me as a writer. From a very early age I saw amazing shows at the Negro Ensemble Company. So I think I was greatly influenced by a lot of those really rich, textured political plays about African American life, and interestingly enough I never felt an absence of our voice in the theatre because it was always there for me.

Hodges: I think, then, for something to have impacted you the way you're saying maybe *A Raisin in the Sun* or *Purlie* did—why do you think specifically those shows or others might have influenced you?

Nottage: I can tell you specifically why *A Raisin in the Sun*. I think that the gift that I have received most often in my life is a copy of *A Raisin in the Sun*. [*Laughs.*] I remember getting the first copy maybe when I was twelve years old from my mother's friend who was a writer. I had expressed an interest in writing, and she gave me a copy of *A Raisin in the Sun*. I can't even remember who she was, but I distinctly remember the gift. Thereafter I would receive a copy of that play as a gift about every three or four years. [*Laughs.*] I would open up the wrapping paper and there it would be. I guess God was trying to send a message to me. As a result I think it is the play that has had the greatest influence on me, as I have read it at just about every phase in my life. I understand why it occupies a space in the literary canon. I remain completely in awe of its craft. I remain in awe of the impact—the social, cultural, and political impact—that it has had on the theatre. It remains a piece of work that inspires me. And I aspire to create something as indelible and human as that play. It is the creative high bar. And I think that Lorraine Hansberry became this fascinating character in my life because I was introduced to her so often by various people at different stages in my life. And at each stage the play took on a new urgency, because I found I identified with the struggles and aspirations of different characters depending on where I was in my own emotional journey. I continue to find new resonance in the play every time I see or read it. It is one of the remarkable aspects of the play—it so thoroughly gives a full voice to each of the characters that you find your sympathies and allegiances constantly shifting and realigning themselves. It is its gift.

Hodges: Everyone else I've spoken to has had the idea that this is what they were going to do and were only encouraged rather than discouraged by seeing other productions. Was that your experience?

Nottage: I have been a prolific reader since I was a child. Good writing has always fueled my desire to write. It is after seeing a truly good production of a play that I feel most driven and jazzed to sit down and write. And so it is not to say that I don't feel intimidated by other writers, because I do feel intimidated every single day of my life. [*Laughs.*] But I use that feeling to challenge myself when I sit down to write. But I also remind myself that I have a set of tools that are unique to my experience, and that allows me to battle the feelings of doubt and insecurity.

Hodges: The other thing that I have seen in my own life as well as the stories of other people who I have spoken to is that *were it not for what was going on in my life at that time*, certain plays might not have had quite as much of an impact. I am wondering whether there were certain plays at certain times that affected your work, when you were developing as a writer?

Nottage: I can tell you. I remember seeing a production of *Mother Courage and Her Children* with Dame Judi Dench in London when I was a junior in college. I was completely broke and I think I had spent my last few pounds to get a seat all the way in the back of the theatre. And the play began and I was just bowled over from the first moment. One, by Judi Dench's masterful performance, but more so by the play itself. It seemed so *muscular*, and it titillated all sides of my brain, if that makes sense. I felt all the synapses going in the same moment. I said, "Oh, I am entertained. Oh, I'm challenged. Oh, I'm moved." The moment which I remember as a transformative moment in the theatre, it's as close as I have ever had to awe, where you gasp and feel something in your body shifting and you don't quite have the language to express what that sensation is. It occurred when Kattrin climbs to the top of the house to warn everyone about the impending danger. And we know that she is mute and she can't say anything, and she opens her mouth and nothing comes out, just this awful silent scream, air, and then she begins clanking the pots and pans. And in that moment, I thought, Oh, gosh, I have so many more tools at my disposal as an artist than I knew. And I am capable of eliciting emotions and doing something that is transformative, and I think that was a revelation for me when I was sitting in the theatre. It was close to the experience of *Succotash on Ice*, when the refrigerator opened and the lima beans begin to speak.

Hodges: You must have felt like that just opened up a whole other world.

Nottage: For me it did. I felt like this great gate had been flung open and I had been permitted for the first time entry to the other side. And I do think that when you have that moment, it's rare and it doesn't happen that often, and it doesn't mean that you haven't seen other theatre that is exceptional and exciting. But I think that that door usually gets opened just once.

Hodges: It seems you were lucky in another sense because you saw the African American experience portrayed onstage, and I don't know how many places there were in the country at that time where it was actually being performed onstage. So you were able to see it, and I am wondering how that affected you because of what else was going on in the world. Your perspective must have been different than that of most people your age.

Nottage: I do think my perspective was probably slightly different, because I grew up in New York City. I grew up with progressive parents who were community activists and who were very open—politically *and* socially. So I think that that left its imprint. I also think that going to theatre at places like the Negro Ensemble made my notion of what belonged on the stage perhaps different from that of mainstream audiences. The first plays I encountered were written by playwrights like Charles Fuller and Micki Grant, and I think that gave me a creative armor, because the theatre that I fell in love with was the sort of theatre that I wanted to make. And it was only when I got to college that I felt the absence of the African American voice on the stage, and it was a curve ball, because I was being told by the academy that the work that I admired and loved was not important enough to study. I had thought, "Oh, all plays are African American plays." I'm joking, of course. But that was my universe for a brief moment. And so when I got to college and read John Osborne and the plays by the angry British playwrights and Chekhov and Ibsen, I thought, Oh, there are other people writing. [*Laughs.*] And so it was kind of the unexpected reversal.

Hodges: Were you seeing shows with mainly black casts?

Nottage: I think, yeah. I had seen predominantly black shows. I had seen shows like *The Me That Nobody Knows* and *Don't Bother Me, I Can't Cope* and *Your Arms Too Short to Box with God* and *Zooman and the Sign* and *The Brownsville Raid* and *The Great MacDaddy* and I was seeing shows at the Billie Holiday Theatre . . . at the Negro Ensemble. When I was growing up my parents would color the pictures of white people in the books brown. [*Laughs.*] So when I was reading the *The Wizard of Oz*, Dorothy was brown. But I also saw *My Fair Lady*, *Merrily We Roll Along*, and many other things.

Hodges: Because you were so conscious about your advantage in seeing so many black faces on the stage, I'm wondering . . .

Nottage: I have to say that I didn't know back then that it was an advantage. Looking back now, I think that it gave me the armor and the confidence to continue writing in an uncensored way. It made me feel my voice was vital.

Hodges: How does that influence you as you write now?

Nottage: I am sure it does impact the way in which I write. How? I am not entirely sure that I have language with which to describe it. But I do think that at least in the last ten years I have felt liberated by my personal history. My writing, as eclectic as it is, is an outgrowth of my life.

Hodges: I have talked to a few people and said, "You know, there are plays that have changed your life and now you are writing plays that are changing other people's lives."

Nottage: Really, that's true. I was talking to someone recently—we had taken a workshop together—and she said, "Do you remember in the workshop what the man said about the soul?" I said, "No, I don't remember." I said, "I remember tons of other things that he said." "But," she said, "do you remember what he said? 'The playwright is a soul healer. We have to think of ourselves in the same way that doctors and lawyers do. That we are absolutely essential to the culture. Because what we are doing is providing some sort of salve, some means for people to go deep inside of themselves and explore emotions, and explore feelings, and to challenge the right and left side of their brains, and then hopefully give them some sort of resolution or at least put them onto the path of resolution and greater understanding of self.'" I said, "That is really beautiful." And I do think that the plays that I was moved by are plays that did and do that.

Hodges: And yours certainly do.

Nottage: Thank, you, I hope that mine do. And I look at *A Raisin in the Sun*. I think that what she did was soul healing, and I think that is why it has become part of the canon. You know, it's that intangible ingredient. I do think that intangible is what a play can do to the soul.

Hodges: I have never heard that expressed that way, and I think it should be more so. People should talk about that, because there's no way to articulate that catharsis sometimes.

Nottage: I think absolutely. I call it "the intangible," and I feel like the good plays—regardless of form or structure—that is what they do.

Hodges: And that may be an explanation for some of those shows that sometimes make you think, I don't have any idea why that affected me like that, because it wasn't that well written. [*Laughs.*]

Nottage: [*Laughs.*] It wasn't that well written, but it gets in there. You don't know why, but it's like "Oh, damn, it's inside. It's doing something!"

14

SUZAN-LORI PARKS

SUZAN-LORI PARKS' plays include *365 Days/365 Plays* (performed over the course of a year in over seven hundred theatres worldwide, creating one of the largest collaborations in theatre history); *Topdog/Underdog* (2002 Pulitzer Prize for Drama); *Fucking A*; *Imperceptible Mutabilities in the Third Kingdom* (1990 Obie Award for Best New American Play); *The America Play*; *Venus* (1996 Obie Award); *The Death of the Last Black Man in the Whole Entire* World; and *In The Blood* (2000 Pulitzer Prize finalist). Her work is the subject of the PBS film *The Topdog Diaries*. Most of Parks' plays are published by Theatre Communications Group. She is an alumna of New Dramatists and has been awarded grants by the National Endowment for the Arts, the Rockefeller Foundation, the Ford Foundation, the New York State Council on the Arts, and the New York Foundation for the Arts. She was also the recipient of a Lila Wallace--Reader's Digest Award, a CalArts/Alpert Award in the Arts (Drama) and a Guggenheim Foundation grant. In 2001 she was awarded a MacArthur Foundation "genius" grant. Her work for the screen includes, as an actor: a leading role in . . . *Plus One,* which premiered at the Cannes Film Festival; as a writer/director: *Anemone Me* (produced by Christine Vachon and Todd Haynes), as a writer: *Girl 6* (directed by Spike Lee), screenplays for Brad Pitt, Jodie Foster, and Denzel Washington, and an adaptation of Zora Neale Hurston's *Their Eyes Were Watching God* (for Oprah Winfrey Presents). Her first novel, *Getting Mother's Body,* is published by Random House. Parts 1, 8, and 9 of her play cycle *Father Comes Home From the Wars* premiered in 2009 at The Public Theater, and the production featured Parks onstage performing songs and guitar accompaniment. Parks currently serves The Public Theater as their Master Writer Chair.

Everything Changes: Your Life

Ben Hodges: Can we talk about your early influences?

Suzan-Lori Parks: These days I'm entertaining a new idea. New for me, anyway. Recently I heard some interesting young writers, wonderful writers, talented folk, saying, "If it hadn't been for so-and-so, I wouldn't have done anything!" Hearing that encouraged me to entertain a different belief system. First, while there are people who grow up in very difficult circumstances and never receive the training or encouragement to help them flower, most of us reading this book probably fall somewhere in the middle. And for those of us who are not in extreme circumstances, believing that, but for a singular spectacular life changing event or teacher, we never would have found ourselves or our path, we might be buying into the idea that there is "something special" out there, and without it you're lost.

Hmm. Talking about the play that changed your life or the teacher who you believe made you a writer is a beautiful opportunity to give thanks to those who helped us along the way. And it also might be sending a constricting message to those who have yet to find that teacher, that path, that singular event. So let's say that maybe the special event doesn't exist. Maybe *every* event, maybe *every* person, is special. Maybe you don't have to get into Harvard to become a success. Maybe the guru is in you. There are a lot of up-and-coming writers these days who believe that they have to get into a certain school or study with a certain writer to become a success, or to become a "real writer."

When writers believe this, they place an expectation on an institution or teacher or external system—and we all know there's a lot of letdown that happens after graduation! Just yesterday (really) on the street a young man came up to me and thanked me for my work and told me that he wouldn't have become a writer if it hadn't been for me. I acknowledged his thanks and then I looked him in the eye and told him what I believe is true: that he would have become a writer with or without me. I wanted him to know that he would have done it. An oak is an oak is an oak. A redwood will be a redwood. Who you are *will out*. You will. You will out yourself. I acknowledge the challenges of people in very difficult circumstances, and—right now speaking to those of us in the middle ground—I want to encourage artists to realize that while teachers, classes, and events can help you, you should not expect them to *make* you. Nor, of course, should the teacher believe that she is *making* the student—but that's a whole other conversation.

Hodges: Someone said to me once that we're where we are doing what we're meant to be doing or we'd be somewhere else doing something else, and so then *that* would be what we're meant to be doing.

Parks: Again, extreme circumstances aside, we choose to be who we will become. We choose ourselves. And we choose every day. We make a choice every day. So that's why it's hard for me to think of the play that changed my life. I mean, it's a totally awesome question to ask and it is a great thing to think about, but in a way I don't know if I really believe, deeply believe, that *if it hadn't been for this, that I wouldn't have become that*. I don't know if I believe that.

But—ah ha! I just thought of something to upset my new belief! Perhaps we can say that if it hadn't been for Abraham Lincoln, I never would have written *The America Play*. Yes—that is true! That is true. Is Abraham Lincoln a play? Abraham Lincoln changed my life! And maybe it was *Our American Cousin* that changed my life. [*Laughs.*] So there we have it! End of interview or should we continue?

Hodges: A lot of people say that they can't point to one thing that led them to playwriting. Were there things in your life—or maybe playwrights—that spoke to you during specific times in your life?

Parks: I think *everything* changes your life. Oh, and that makes it all so "awful but cheerful," as Elizabeth Bishop would say. Yes, every encounter is life changing. Oh, that means that *everybody* is important. Darn, right? There's no special V.I.P. section! Or if there is, we're all velvet-snaked up in it! Rumi says that every encounter produces a child. Every encounter is that important. And this also is true: I've had wonderful writing teachers along the way.

In the early 1980s I took a writing class with James Baldwin, the wonderful novelist, essayist, and playwright. He encouraged me to go into playwriting. Would I have *not* gone into playwriting if it had not been for James Baldwin? To be honest, I probably would've eventually found my way into playwriting, because my short stories already so closely resembled playwriting. I might not have joined the theatre that *day*, as I did when he suggested it. Maybe I would have done it the next year. I was already in love with Shakespeare. This is also true: I've seen loads of great productions, among them Ariane Mnouchkine's *Les Atrides* (*The House of Atreus*). I've also read wonderful plays and books like Adrienne Kennedy's *People Who Led to My Plays*.

Hodges: Everyone comes to writing in different ways at different times. But Nilo Cruz, for instance, hadn't seen any plays before he was in his teens. When did you first see a play?

Parks: Well, that would be the third grade when I was a squirrel in the Thanksgiving pageant. [*Laughs.*] I guess I didn't *see* the play because I was *in* the play.

My dad was a real opera fan—he would sing opera around the house. He was really tall, so that was a show right there—my dad singing along with Verdi. So there's theatre there. For my mom's birthday this past year, we sur-

The Chorus of the 1992 Théâtre du Soleil and Brooklyn Academy of Music production of Les Atrides (House of Atreus), *the four-play, ten-hour cycle of Greek tragedy directed by Ariane Mnouchkine, at the 14th Street Regiment Armory in Brooklyn, New York. (Photo by Martine Franck/Magnum Photos, courtesy of the Brooklyn Academy of Music)*

prised her by taking her to see the Broadway production of *Hair*. At the end of the show, of course, we got her up onstage to dance. And she had a surprise for me too: she gave me her copy of the original cast album. She and Dad had seen the Broadway show in the '60s. He was in the army at the time. Deep.

Hodges: How did you get started going to the theatre here in New York and what did you think about it?

Parks: Cheap. [*Laughs.*] Cheap. When I moved to New York I didn't have any money so I went to shows that didn't cost much.

Hodges: You saw the fringe shows, the Off-Off-Broadway shows?

Parks: Yeah. Plus Shakespeare in the Park cause it was free. To be honest, there wasn't much on Broadway I was dying to see anyway. Broadway is cool, but my heart is downtown.

Hodges: I know aspiring writers sometimes think, "I couldn't do that." What made you think you could do it, and when?

Parks: I never thought that I couldn't do it. I only thought about how I wanted to do it, and how I loved it. I worked a temp job, I self-produced, and I also went around trying to get productions. That is how I ended up at BACA Downtown. After seeing a show at Franklin Furnace one night, there was a woman from the audience on the train. I asked her if she knew of any hip places that produced plays. She suggested BACA Downtown. And I didn't know it at the time, but she was Alisa Solomon [of the *Village Voice*]. Mac Wellman was the dramaturg there. He read *Imperceptible Mutabilities of the Third Kingdom* and suggested BACA produce it. The show won the Obie Award for Best New American Play, along with one of Mac's plays and a play by Craig Lucas—we all three won.

I started hanging out at BACA because they welcomed me. It wasn't because I wanted to be downtown and avant-garde. I just wanted to get my plays done. I self-produced my New York premiere at the Gas Station and had a wonderful time. But then I thought, Well, it might be nice to get produced—because people *do* get plays done, you know, at venues where they have programming. [*Laughs.*] In some ways my big break was when I did my own play, self-produced, and I paid everybody and all that.

Hodges: I didn't know that self-producing aspect of your early years.

Parks: Oh, yeah. My very first play in New York was at The Gas Station. *Betting on The Dust Commander*, about two people who bet on a horse called The Dust Commander. It's actually the name of a real horse. And Laurie Carlos, who is a wonderful writer and performance artist, was in the original *for colored girl who have considered suicide/when the rainbow is enuf*, she directed the play. Everybody got paid a little.

I am proud of that because I was saying, "I value your time, and I'm willing to take earnings from my temp job and pay you. That was the only money I had, from my little temp job. The Gas Station was a bar that used to be a gas station. It had one couch in it as furniture—a green couch on which all kinds of things happened. It had Christmas lights hanging that would blink on and off and on and off. And I would go there and hang out at like three in the morning and watch the Christmas lights go blink, blink . . . blink, blink. And one night I asked, "You guys ever do plays here?" And the bartender/owner was like, "Hey! Yeah, we could! You go buy some lights, and we'll buy some chairs," he said. So I went to the hardware store and bought some silver clip-on lights and two long industrial-strength yellow extension cords. He bought some chairs, like twenty plastic lawn chairs, and we did my play, and three people came—my mom, my dad, and a homeless guy that lived outside. No kidding, I had a three-day run, which was the standard run for the Off-Off-Off-Off-Off-Off-Off-Off-Off-Off-Off-Off-Off-Off-Off-Broadway theatre. You know, three days. It had a slideshow in it too.

I'm still into slides and photographic stuff with theatre. Still doing it, like right now with *Father Comes Home From the Wars*. I did it in *Imperceptible Mutabilities*. . . . Anyway, my job during *Dust Commander* was to sit behind a screen, not visible to the audience; I had an extension cord in each hand, and "lights down" was unplug the extension cords and "lights up" was plugging in the extension cords—in-out, in-out, in-out, for the hour and a half. It didn't have an intermission. [*Laughs*.] So that was my first show in New York. I really felt that I had arrived. We pretty much self-produced *365 Days/365 Plays*. Bonnie Metzgar and Rebecca Rugg, me and David Myers, we went around nationally and internationally and banded together this awesome worldwide network of artists and we all produced it together. And all the performances were free of charge. Self-producing can be very cool. But a writer should remember that regardless of production opportunities, she can always write—you gotta make up your mind early on: I'm going to write regardless—because I'm a *writer*.

Hodges: But you couldn't have relied on that or you wouldn't have been writing very long.

Parks: Who can know? A lot of writers *do* rely on that. It takes a beautiful strength. A lot of poets write and write and don't get published much. They have a beautiful certainty. The rest of us need more encouragement. And we need "North Stars."

There are lots of writers I look up to: Ntozake Shange, Adrienne Kennedy. . . . But I don't just take my role models from black women who write plays, although there are awesome and fearless women who do. Or black women who write, although there are awesome and fearless women who do. I take my role models from whoever is great at what they do. That's who I look to. My North Star might be an awesome black woman or a dead white man. I don't care, you know? I want to be as good as I possibly can at what I do. So I look to the people who are as good as they possibly are.

When I was coming up, I was like, "Ntozake Shange's great." Also Edward Albee is great. Shakespeare's great. Sophocles is great. August Wilson's great. So is Sam Shepard, so is Tennessee Williams, so is Euripides, Ed Bullins, and—the list goes on and on. I was looking up to the awesome ones. Those are the footsteps I want to walk in. They could be Black or Asian or Latino or Greek or dead or whatever. I don't care. Certainly when you find someone "like you," that might be helpful, but ultimately, at the end of the day, who is like you *really*? Then you suddenly realize, "Oh, gee, I'm *me*."

Hodges: Do writers emulate other writers' structure, or do they say, "I can't write like that, I have to do it *this way*"? Or "This is the way *I* write"? Or is it just, "I write. I'm not going to worry about structure"? Or with you is it something a bit peculiar because you are, I'm not even going to use that word "unconventional"—do you worry about how it is going to be produced?

Parks: Well, I think those are two different sets of questions. One—structure. And two—what's going to happen to it after I write it? For me, structure is what's happening as I'm writing it, right? How am I shaping it? And in that respect I feel like I'm in a tradition of nontraditional writers. I can also write a two-character play that takes place in a room. Cool. Let me be clear: I don't *set out* to write unconventional plays because I *want to be* unconventional. I was talking to some young writer, and they asked me: "So before you write, do you like, say, OK, I have to break the mold?" And I was like, "You're outta your mind!"

Hodges: But some people think that's what you do.

Parks: I know! And I don't. For the record, I don't. I don't do that. I sit down and I go, "Gee, I want to write a play." If it's a play. If it's a novel—I have written a novel, and I am working on my second one—I think, "Gee, I want to write a novel." Or if it's a song—which I am writing right now, my guitar is sitting there, the lyrics to a song from *Father Comes Home From the Wars* are half-written right there—I say "Gee, I want to write a song." That's all I say. And then I sit down and get to work. I just want to write something. I'm not a picky mother—I'm not stressing on what the baby looks like. I'm sampling, recycling, helping to relay the tradition, but—I'm not even conventional within my own conventions—but that is what I mean about each new experience being life changing. Every experience is life changing. If you recognize the "importance of the special," put that alongside the "specialness of the everyday"—they're equally important.

I haven't yet figured out what "a Suzan-Lori Parks play" looks like. I haven't decided forever on *my style*. I'm just trying to write something. To tell the story as best I can. I haven't yet said: *I know how to write plays now. Today I am going to cross my arms and put my feet up on my desk and write like this forever.* Not. The play I wrote in 1990 doesn't look much like the play I wrote in 1999. It doesn't look like the play I wrote in 2009. *Father Comes Home From the Wars* doesn't look like *The Death of the Last Black Man in the Entire World* and *Topdog* doesn't look like *Imperceptible Mutabilities* and *Fucking A* doesn't look like *Topdog*. They're all their own creatures. And whassup with *365Days/365Plays*! Oh my God, write a play a day for a whole year then produce it in over 700 venues!? Hey, it was fun! Playtime. So the structure when you're writing is one thing for me. How I am shaping this? How am I telling the story? That's the structure. That's question number 1. The next part—after you are done writing it—is, How will it get produced? That's a *whole* other second phase of it. I don't think about how it's getting produced when I'm writing it.

Hodges: At any point in your life when you go see another playwright or a play, or you're reading a Tennessee Williams play, which seems to have one basic kind of structure . . .

Parks: Kind of. But then there's *Camino Real*. I read that and I was like, "Whoo-hoo!" I'm like, "Right on, brother. Break out of your own mold. Break out of your own comfort zone!" I'm so proud of him for writing that.

Hodges: I assume you have long since stopped, if you ever did, comparing yourself to other writers that you have read or seen or how they affect how you work now.

Parks: I'm always interested in what other writers are making. There are lots of great playwrights these days. I see a lot of shows. Although, sometimes when I go see a play, I never want to have anything to do the theatre ever again. And that lasts for about five minutes. And then I call a friend, kind of like they suggest you do in Alcoholics Anonymous, and you go, "Friend, I just saw a play that made me never what to have anything to do the theatre again." And they say, "Well, don't worry, it will pass." And you say, "Really?" And they say, "Remember when I called you yesterday and said the same thing to you?" And you say, "Oh, yeah, you're right." Okay. And you go for a walk and by the time you've rounded the block you realize that you've found a way to continue.

Hodges: It that because it was bad?

Parks: Bad, good—who can know?

Some plays are not fun to watch but they are enormously healing for the people involved in creating them. Some plays make great shows but are horrible experiences for the players. And some plays—well, they may make money, but they don't really lift the spirit or enlighten the soul. That's not the definition of great theatre, but those are the kinds of shows I enjoy. It doesn't turn a mirror onto you. It doesn't do all those great things that theatre can do. It might wag a finger at you for an hour and a half and tell you something "very important." It might be a play about an important subject that it is poorly written, which is unfortunate.

I tell my students that Van Gogh is not a great painter because he chose a great subject. Van Gogh is not a great painter because he painted kings. Van Gogh is a great painter because he had a high level of craft, and it is not enough to write a play about an important *topic*. You must write with a high level of *craft*. Some people think, "Well, I'll just write about something important and my play will be important." That is *not* correct. But at the end of the day, aside from whether or not I *like* a show, I enjoy going. It's important to sit in the crowd and feel that "Go team!" moment. "Go team!" It's *always* that, regardless of the quality, really.

Sometimes you go to a football game and your team is so . . . ugh! You never want to go to another game. Same kind of thing. I went to a Knicks game a couple of months ago. It was *heartbreaking*. You don't want to go to another Knicks game but *they're all there*. You know, it's a "Go team!" moment. So you do the same thing with theatre. I do, anyway. I go to lots and lots of plays. I always encourage the writer and encourage the production. We gotta spread the Love, right?

15

SARAH RUHL

SARAH RUHL's plays include *The Clean House* (Susan Smith Blackburn Prize, 2004; Pulitzer Prize finalist; PEN American Center Award); *Melancholy Play*; *Eurydice*; *Late: a cowboy song*; *Orlando*; *Demeter in the City* (NAACP Image Award nomination); *Passion Play* (Kennedy Center Fourth Forum Freedom Award); *Dead Man's Cell Phone* (Helen Hayes Award); and *In the Next Room (or the vibrator play)*. Her plays have been performed at Lincoln Center Theater, Second Stage, Playwrights Horizons, the Goodman Theatre, Yale Repertory Theatre, Woolly Mammoth, Berkeley Repertory Theatre, the Wilma Theater, the Cornerstone Theater, Madison Repertory Theatre, the Clubbed Thumb, and the Piven Theatre Workshop, as well as other theatres across the country. They have been translated into German, Polish, Korean, Russian, and Spanish, and have been produced internationally in London, Canada, Germany, Latvia, and Poland. Ruhl, who is originally from Chicago, received her master's degree in fine arts from Brown University. She is the recipient of a Helen Merrill Award, a Whiting Writers' Award, a PEN/Laura Pels Foundation Award, and a MacArthur Fellowship ("genius grant"). She is a proud member of New Dramatists and 13P.

Photo by © Walter McBride/Retna Ltd.

The Baltimore Waltz *and the plays of my childhood*

I first saw Paula Vogel's *The Baltimore Waltz* at Brown University when I was nineteen. It was a tiny student production in a black-box theatre that used to be a cafeteria; there were empty refrigerators in the wings. The smallness of the place might not have led one to anticipate the largeness of the evening's impact. Plays, in general, are not like novels—something to curl up with in bed, a paper thing to befriend. It is one of their shortcomings, plays—they are not terribly fun to read in bed, or to read in the bath, to be loved over time,

Left to right: Richard Thompson as Carl, Cherry Jones as Anna, and Joe Mantello as The Third Man in the 1992 Circle Repertory Company production of Paula Vogel's The Baltimore Waltz. *(Photo by Gerry Goodstein, courtesy of the John Willis Theatre World/ Screen World Archive)*

put down, picked up, dog-eared. They do not replace human conversation at the breakfast table. They decimate you in the moment, and then they are gone, a flash in the pan, a memory. But Paula's play decimated me in the moment, and then, somehow, over time, became a friend.

I came to see the play before I knew Paula. (How is it that I ever did not know Paula? I can scarcely remember such a state of being. . . .) At any rate, the twenty-year-old director of *The Baltimore Waltz* in the Russell Lab at Brown University in 1993 made some choices that in retrospect I can't imagine Paula loving—like painting the face of Anna white, a nod to commedia, or expressionism, I suppose. But it did give the production a stylized feeling and reminded me of death masks. The fellow playing The Third Man was named Sasha, I believe, and he was very hairy, and a very good comic actor. The actor playing Carl was a tall, thin undergraduate with large eyes. The set was nothing much—a black box with white hospital sheets hung up on a line as curtains, and a gurney. I went with a good friend who had lost her father to AIDS in the '80s. My own father, during that autumn, was dying of cancer in Chicago. I was something of a sleepwalker at college, not quite understanding the concerns of most nineteen-year-olds, and always on my way home to Chicago, always on some empty sun-drenched flight home, when I wasn't madly writing a paper on the imagery of curtains in the gothic novel in order to forget.

My friend and I sat through *The Baltimore Waltz* rapt. During the final moment, when Anna and Carl waltz, never to go on their trip to Europe, but permitted one last dance—in the afterlife, perhaps, or in the theatre . . . or in memory—I was racked with sobs. The audience left, and my friend and I sat there, sobbing, two young women who had been around too many deathbeds for our age. (In medieval Europe, of course, we'd have been incredibly lucky to have lost only our fathers.)

Things I may have unconsciously absorbed from *The Baltimore Waltz*: How Paula created a modern architecture for grief. How she transmuted personal loss into something formal, and how she both stepped back from the grief formally, but laid the grief bare in an extraordinary, transparent way at the end. How Paula laughs at terrible, terrible things. How she uses gesture and language in that play, and how there was no fourth wall. How she used fragment. How she changed modes and styles quickly, seamlessly. How language itself can be a source of solace but also a mode of alienation. How the personal can coexist up against the iconic and become even more personal for the contrast. How she includes what you might call a relic in the work—she includes a beautiful letter from her brother Carl in the program note—and what her insistence on the real means about art—how arbitrary are our distinctions between the real and the unreal. How she sees theatre as a place for memory, and for ghosts.

Later, when Paula came to be my teacher, she would give me a rubric for understanding some of what she did in *The Baltimore Waltz* (although no cold theoretical rubric could ever explain what it is that she does in her work.) Paula speaks often of "Russian Formalism" and lectures on Viktor Shklovsky. His notion is that art defamiliarizes the familiar; art aims to make driving seem strange even though it is an automatic thing that we do in life. Paula

Kathleen Ruhl (Sarah Ruhl's mother-to-be) as Sarah Brown in the 1969 Music Theatre of Hyde Park production of Guys and Dolls *in Chicago, Illinois. (Photo by Pat Ruhl)*

defamiliarizes driving in *How I Learned to Drive*; she defamiliarizes disease in *The Baltimore Waltz*. As a young woman watching my father being wheeled in and out of hospitals, the act of making disease strange in order to see it newly was both emotionally raw and intellectually accurate. The modern alienation from disease and death—the search for a ritual response to death rather than a medical model—was something I would turn to again and again in my own work.

When I finally did meet Paula in a writing class, after having sobbed my pants off at her play, and after having lost my father, I thought, listening to her lecture (as Gertrude Stein wrote that Alice B. Toklas said upon meeting Gertrude Stein), This is the first genius I have ever met. And I think there was something about meeting Paula, and having been so affected by her work, that made it possible for me to write. That is to say, I always wrote—as a young child I wrote poems, and stories and plays—but that meeting Paula made it possible for me to take up what is known rather ponderously as the writing life. I wonder if one precondition for taking on writing as an absolute vocation is to realize that the great works you so admire were written by living people—not given to Moses on the mountaintop, not flung down onto parchment from great heights, but written by people who eat cookies or offer cookies or talk on the telephone. And not only written by people in general, but yes, also written by women. Even if I had never met Paula (and if I had never met Paula, I would now probably still be writing papers about the imagery of curtains in the gothic novel), seeing that one play of hers would still have been a revelatory gift. I think there is something alchemical in her process—she creates sites for the audience for mourning—particularly in *How I Learned to Drive*, *The Baltimore Waltz*, and *The Long Christmas Ride Home*. For an audience to be given a place to mourn—this is at the root of why we make theatre, in an ancient, ancient way—but sometimes it feels like a distant art now, in an era of more glossy, emotionally reconstituted work.

I want to digress for a moment to my theatregoing days before *The Baltimore Waltz*, to the plays of my childhood. Because I think that the plays I saw in my childhood, especially the ones I saw repeatedly in childhood, prepared me for seeing *The Baltimore Waltz*. My mother was an actress in Chicago in the '60s, working on plays by people like Maria Irene Fornes and Megan Terry, and when two children came along, my mother suspended acting in the city and did community theatre in the suburbs where we lived. And she taught English at a Catholic high school, where she also directed plays. I saw many plays in my childhood, but the plays I saw over and over again were *Enter Laughing, A Midsummer Night's Dream,* and *Romeo and Juliet.*

My mother directed *Enter Laughing* at the Wilmette Community Theater when I was seven or eight years old. For some reason this play entered my imagination so fully that I was crushed when the run ended. Harry Tienowitz, an awkward young actor with a lisp, played David, the hapless would-be actor who walks into an audition and, misreading the stage direction for dialogue, says, "Enter laughing." And thus: *Enter Laughing* might have given me a taste for what I might call boulevard humor. And for plays about plays. David later says to Angela Marlowe (his sophisticated-actress love interest), "You're a better man than I am, Gunga Din," in a failed attempt to prove to her his poetic nature. My sister and I repeated this line over and over, finding it hilarious. "You're a better man than I am, Gunga Din," cackle, cackle. We had no idea what it meant. I still don't. Perhaps this gave me my first taste for language that seemed to have meaning in sound divorced from content. Language that felt absurd even when an eight-year-old couldn't locate, in a literary sense, why it was absurd. I found the actress who played Angela Marlowe horribly, painfully glamorous, both onstage and off—the slow way she put on her stockings in her dressing room, and the way she would smoke on her breaks. So I was given this early sense that there was a halo of glamour around theatre, even at the Wilmette Community Theater, where dentists played heroes and businessmen played dentists. I took notes in the back, in the dark of the theatre, watching most rehearsals, and giving my notes to my mother the director, who was very receptive and often passed my notes on to her actors. (This formative experience might make me trying to directors even now during tech.) I saw many rehearsals and many performances of *Enter Laughing,* and when I learned that my mother and father were going to closing night, and my sister and I were to be left home with a sitter, I felt wretched and betrayed. The betrayal was not only missing the last performance; it was also that I didn't know I was seeing the play for the last time when I saw it, and so I wasn't able to fully appreciate it, couldn't properly savor every moment as the last. I cried on the floor of the living room, bereft, as my mother and father walked out the door.

The second production that was etched into my prehensile mind was a production of *A Midsummer Night's Dream* at Regina Dominican High School, also directed by my mother. She set it in the '20s, and there were flappers and gangsters. I believe the rustics were gangsters and the fairies were flappers. There were also ballet dancers. One of the fairies danced en pointe. Seeing *Midsummer* over and over again gave me a taste for Shakespeare's linguistic melodies, for his songs, and for his magic. And perhaps there was something about the production being set in the modern world—about the ability to bring together the ancient and the modern. People have often asked me whether I ally myself with the magical realists—and I do love Márquez and am flattered to be in his company—but I think it is really Shakespeare's romances where I found an early love of theatrical magic and transformation. To this day, I love best Shakespeare's romances and tragedies. His histories and his comedies I appreciate, but not with the same lust.

And so on to tragedy. *Romeo and Juliet* at North Shore Community Theater—with my mother playing the nurse, directed, as I recall, by the grand pooh-bah of North Shore Community Theater, a rotund, theatrical man with a beard and a booming voice named Ron Tobas. Every night my mother howled in grief over the apparently lifeless body of her charge. It was strange to see my mother howl in grief. To see her in such theatrical distress. "My lamb! My lady!" as she collapsed over a body. I had dreams, as a twelve-year-old, that I had to go on as Juliet. And when I cried at the play, I cried for Juliet, but more, I cried for my mother crying for Juliet. Which perhaps gave me a displaced point of view, of who the main character might actually be in a tragedy.

How did *Enter Laughing*, *A Midsummer Night's Dream*, and *Romeo and Juliet* prepare me for the work of Paula Vogel? I think Paula and I both share a love for high and low, for the mixing of genres, for the love of language itself, for transformation, and for populism, all of which you see in those three plays. I think it's also significant that these formative productions weren't necessarily the best, in the professional sense of the word. I do think they were all very good productions in their way (or they are in my subjective memory of them), but they were not, for instance, Glenn Close on Broadway, or the Goodman Theatre's *A Christmas Carol*, both of which I saw at an early age, and which may have had an effect, but a dim one. The productions that moved me most were born of small communities—a high school, a university, and straight-up *community theatre*—one of the most detested compound words in the annals of professional theatre.

Part of why these productions may have had an effect on me was sheer repetition—seeing something over and over again until it is part of you. But also, I have no doubt, I was affected by seeing work born of people I was related to, or knew casually. What is more moving than seeing someone you love onstage, or better yet, watching someone watch someone they love onstage? The watcher is lit up, transformed, suddenly infinitely more interesting than the person onstage. These were not professional actors, professional directors, hired guns coming in from New York and putting up something sleek and lovely in Chicago or in Providence. (And I did see my share of those productions, as I would later see, by contrast, my share of productions growing organically out of the ensemble theatre movement in Chicago: the Piven Theatre Workshop, Steppenwolf, Lookingglass, which all had an impact, as did working with Cornerstone Theater, years later.)

I think there is something about the way Paula sees community, and sees theatre growing out of small, tight-knit groups, that feels absolutely necessary to me in terms of the continuance of the form. Why do people go to plays on Broadway? For many reasons, one being that perhaps they played the (narrator) Stage Manager in *Our Town* in third grade. Why do people take their children to *A Christmas Carol*? Perhaps because they played the angel in their church nativity play, or because they played Clarence Darrow in high school, or because their mother sewed costumes for community theatre, as did Peachy Taylor, who made all the costumes for the North Shore Community Theater. And why do we go to community theatre? Not because the reviews were good, but because *we have to*—because the person we know who is involved would be *offended* if we didn't—we go, in other words, because of the social contract, and the ticket prices are minimal or nonexistent. The contract that binds the audience to the work is nonmaterial and not terribly aesthetic—it is based on social ties. The play is an occasion to exercise social bonds, rather than the other way around.

I say all this because it seems significant to me that after all the mesmerizing professional productions I've seen, after all the work of all the virtuosic actors I've seen, it was a student production of *The Baltimore Waltz*, inside a black box that used to be a cafeteria that was later shut down because of asbestos on the ceiling, with actors who are now probably all in advertising—it was *this* production that still moves me to tears when I think of it. And remembering such productions reminds me that the theatre cannot be reduced to once-a-month luxuries for professionals. And when I think of Paula's work I am reminded that the concept of *play itself*—the open, playful, quality of her work—is a primary process, not a luxury, not a hobby, but something all children must do to survive into adulthood.

When I watch my toddler play, and she is at one moment a self-proclaimed mean turtle and then a nice turtle and then a grown man, each fiercely and completely, it reminds me of the primary human hope that identity might in fact be fluid, that we are simultaneously ourselves and the beasts in the field, a donkey, a queen, a starlet, a lover—and that identity might be nothing more than dipping our Heraclitan feet in the river, moment to moment. And if identity is fluid, then we might actually be free. And furthermore, if identity is fluid, then we might actually be connected—in Whitman's sense—if we can be the leaves of grass and also the masses on the Brooklyn Bridge, then we can leave the ego behind and be world for a moment. And this is one reason why we go to theatre: either to identify with others, or to *be* others, for the moment; and in what we call community theatre, the identification might be stronger, because we are more likely to either play the donkey ourselves, or to know the donkey intimately.

I do not mean to write here a treatise on my preference for community theatre over and above professional theatre—clearly I spend more time in professional theatre than I do anywhere else, which I suppose makes professional theatre my community—my version of community theatre. But what I mean to say is, the productions that have had the biggest impact on me have ferreted their way into the most porous, childlike parts of me, winnowed in and stayed there—and so the most primary among them have also been the smallest in scale. Smallness is subversive, because smallness can creep into smaller places, and smallness can then wreak transformation at the most vulnerable, cellular level. I wish to remember the beauty of smallness. And of proximity. In a time when largeness is threatening to topple us—I want to remember the Davids of theatre, and the Goliath of loneliness. Thank you, Paula, thank you, Mom and Shakespeare, thank you, Ron Tobas and Joyce Piven and Angela Marlowe and Peachy Taylor and Harry Tienowitz, for making me less lonely in this terribly large world.

16

....

JOHN PATRICK SHANLEY

Photo by Monique Carboni

JOHN PATRICK SHANLEY's plays include *Defiance, Danny and the Deep Blue Sea, Savage in Limbo, the dreamer examines his pillow, Beggars in the House of Plenty, Welcome to the Moon, Four Dogs and a Bone, Italian American Reconciliation, The Big Funk, Where's My Money, Dirty Story, Sailor's Song*, and *Romantic Poetry* (a musical). His play *Doubt* was awarded the 2005 Pulitzer Prize for Drama and the 2005 Tony Award for Best Play. In the arena of film, Shanley has had four spec screenplays produced: *Five Corners, Moonstruck, The January Man*, and *Joe Versus the Volcano. Five Corners* won the Special Jury Prize for its screenplay at the Barcelona Theatre Festival. For *Moonstruck*, Shanley received both the Academy Award and the Writers Guild of America Award for Best Original Screenplay. He also did the film adaptations of *Alive* and *Congo*, as well as *Live From Baghdad* for HBO. Shanley directs in both theatre and film. His adaptation of *Doubt*, which he directed, was nominated for an Academy Award for Best Adapted Screenplay. The film stars Meryl Streep, Philip Seymour Hoffman, Amy Adams, and Viola Davis, all of whom were nominated for Academy Awards for their performances.

Standing in the Wings

Ben Hodges: Not knowing what you were going to mention prior to this interview, hopefully there was a play or plays that changed your life . . .

John Patrick Shanley: Until I was twenty-two years old, I only saw two plays. And they were both at Cardinal Spellman High School in the Bronx. Student productions. But they were *excellent* productions, and they were in a facility which, at that time, was a $1 million theatre. So the production values were kind of extraordinary, and the plays were *The Miracle Worker* and *Cyrano de Bergerac*. *The Miracle Worker* I saw probably when I was twelve, right before I went to that school. My brother was on the stage crew there. And then *Cyrano de Bergerac* I saw from the wings, because I was on the stage crew the following year, and as a result I saw and heard the play repeatedly, and that had a huge effect on me. *The Miracle Worker* did too, but I only saw it once. And just the sheer power of the storytelling of *The Miracle Worker* blew me away. But then when I saw *Cyrano*—here was a poet who was the toughest guy in the room, and the most terrific guy and the most romantic guy and a freak at the same time. So I really identified with him and the beauty of the language, and I would say that *Cyrano* was one of the biggest influences on my writing life. And also that relationship of standing in the wings in relation to a play rather than being onstage or being in the audience. Being very close to the material, but at the same time neither the recipient nor the performer. But I was in that third role, I guess, which turned out to be the playwright.

Hodges: So already, that young, you feel like for years afterward that influenced your writing even though you hadn't, I assume, been writing much at all?

Shanley: No, I won my first writing prize when I was eleven, for a Catholic essay contest, the Moody Essay Contest. And I used to mention this from time to time in this context and that, and I mentioned it when I was shooting *Doubt* and my technical advisor, Sister Peggy, who had been my first grade schoolteacher, said, "Oh, I won the Moody Essay Contest when I was a kid." And I was like, "Really?" The only other person I had ever heard knowing of it had also been one of the winners of it. So I was writing poetry and little stories from the time I was ten or eleven. And I did not see *Cyrano de Bergerac* and think, "This is what I want to do." I thought, "This who I want to *be*." The idea of a warrior poet—*that* I found very attractive. And also Ragueneau, who is the pastry chef in that play, and who would give the cavaliers pastries in exchange for poetry—that idea really appealed to me. That poetry had that kind of value, and that there were people in the world, practical people, like bakers, who recognized that value and were willing to give their work in exchange for that work. That really struck me as well. So I've always really liked the character of Ragueneau a lot.

Hodges: Do you think that it's certain plays at certain times? And also, you can go see a movie if you're not in a good mood and maybe you could watch it again later and you may have a different reaction to it, but plays are not necessarily like that—sometimes you have only one shot to see a show.

Shanley: I think that is really true. I think that one of the peculiar things about my exposure to *Cyrano* was that I was being exposed at the same time to the incredible artifice of the theatre, because I was standing behind the painted flats watching from the wings, often along with the actors who were about to go on. All of us talking in whispers like we were in church.

Hodges: And you could not really hear what was going on in the play itself?

Shanley: In a way. But in other words, I was aware of the artifice, and in fact, the artifice enhanced the experience for me. The technical side of it, the colored lights, the painted flats, that was part of it for me. Not simply that I forgot all that stuff and was just wrapped up in the story of *Cyrano*. I was wrapped up in the painted flats and the colored lights and the guys onstage in makeup with big noses and stuff who were reciting poetry. And also the idea of being involved, to have poetry be a popular form, rather than what it was when I was a kid, which was useless. That was very attractive to me, because I was writing poetry.

Hodges: Were you intimidated back then by the high level of theatre that you were participating in and surrounded by in New York?

Shanley: No, I wasn't intimidated because I did not really have any particular knowledge that I was going to do this, first of all. And second of all, even if I did it . . . you know, later, when I was writing constantly, I still had no idea that I could do this for a living. I just—I never met another artist. I grew up in a place . . . none of the people in my family went into the arts. No one in my neighborhood had ever gone into the arts. I am the only one of five children who ever graduated from college. There was no role model—except Cyrano. There was something so far removed from my daily life that I did not even worry about that. And I did later on, you know, when I was a struggling playwright, when I was just starting out, and I had done a couple of plays at New York University when I was a student, and then I went out into the world. And I went to see a play. I had seen the review in the newspaper of a drama—the kind of play that's never produced commercially any more. But it was a drama about a family who had a kid who had some physiological problems and how they dealt with that, and it was a good review, a very nice review. So I got free tickets and I went to see this play. It had an intermission, and I was watching the play and it occurred to me: I could write better than this. And I knew it. I could write better than this. And what I didn't know was that during that act it had begun to snow, and so when I went outside the world was changed. At intermission I remember stepping outside and seeing that the world had changed. And the world inside me had changed, because

I suddenly knew something about what I could do, strangely, from seeing somebody else's work.

Hodges: I am wondering more about how you identified with Cyrano.

Shanley: I completely identify with Cyrano. Because I felt like a freak. I felt like, here I was, and I was a poet, and I was sort of born that way. And also I had the additional feeling of just being a teenager, and all teenagers feel like freaks. And that is like having an abnormally long nose, and it is a question of whether or not somebody is going to make fun of you for your difference. And in Cyrano's case, basically saying, "My difference is what makes me great," and finding a way to embrace that, even though, in Cyrano's case, his difference means that he will never find love. I think we all have that concern. I think when you're thirteen years old and you're in detention six days a week and you never see the light of day and everybody is telling you that you're no good, yeah, you have that concern. And you don't feel as loved. [*Laughs.*]

Hodges: How much of an escape was it for you, especially being from a completely different world, as you say you were. Okay, sure, it was a different world, and it opened up into a world for you, but were there other elements that appealed to you because it was antithetical to what you had been doing?

Shanley: Well, I thought, and I still think, that *Cyrano* is the real world and that the agreed-upon reality that so many of us share is a pallid mask hiding your beautiful face.

Hodges: Actually, I feel the older I get, the more theatre seems like fun, and the more we make of the game, the more fun it is. And maybe that is all it is meant to do, and maybe that is enough.

Shanley: No, I don't feel that way. And as I said, you know, like when I was on the stage crew and we all had to speak in very low voices, with low little red lights or green lights backstage, it felt like church. You know, you had to be quiet. And then there was this sort of central ceremony going on, and the same kind of audience where the congregation is and all that. But it seemed to me that whereas the Roman Catholic Church that I was raised in seemed long dead—the ritual, *this* seemed to be very much alive, and talking about the things that did connect us to the stars.

Hodges: And because you were sort of in and around New York City, do you know what the first Broadway show was that you saw—the first one that had such an impact?

The 1964 production of Edmond Rostand's Cyrano de Bergerac *at Cardinal Spellman High School in the Bronx, New York. (Photo courtesy of Cardinal Spellman High School, Bronx, New York)*

Shanley: My first wife was what they called a second-night critic. And so there was the list of the first-night critics, and there were the second-night critics. She was film critic for a cable TV show, and I remember her telling me that when she would be doing her segments that the cameras got really hot and the cameramen would be cooking TV dinners on top of the cameras and so she would be smelling the fish sticks while she was giving her review. [*Laughs.*] So when I was twenty-two, suddenly I saw a lot of movies and a lot of plays, and I saw a whole season of Lincoln Center. I remember things like *The Plough and the Stars*, and a Gorky play, which was *Enemies*, and a Chekhov play, and some really failed plays, and then I saw David Rabe's *In the Boom Boom Room*, with Madeline Kahn, and then *Streamers*, which he did after that. So I got exposed to a lot of different kinds of theatre, all on a fairly grand scale—the big stages, right after that. This was the mid '70s.

Hodges: Did you feel that that was the place that you wanted your work to debut?

Shanley: It had never occurred to me. Even when I started to write plays, which I did two year or three years later, I did not picture those stages as where I would do this. I saw really a three-hundred-seat house. And since then I think it has gone down to fifty seats in my head.

Hodges: And way the economy is going, that's not such a bad ambition.

Shanley: Yeah, I know it. You know, the great thing about the economy is that the golden age of American playwrights was the 1930s. It was a different time. And the stimulus bill—I wish it did have something included for the arts in that sense, where they funded people by doing plays, basically. Which is a great thing. It's a great thing for the morale of New York City, as well as from the actors' and writers' points of view, but also from the audiences' point of view. People are going to need to go out and have positive, communal experiences during this long winter.

Hodges: I realized when I started doing this that some playwrights will have already touched so many people's lives. Do you ever think about that? Or do you still sort of feel like the guy who's trying to write the next . . .

Shanley: You're always the guy trying to write the next . . .

Hodges: How does it land on you that there are going to be Pulitzer Prize-winning playwrights who say you were the reason they wanted to become a playwright?

Shanley: I've heard those kinds of things and I say, "Thank you." [*Laughs.*] When I was a kid in the Bronx, and I did not know which way to go and I didn't have anybody to tell me which way to go, I did pick up a trail that had been left by others before me. It was literature. People write things and they die. And the stuff they leave behind is the road for the future, for the next generation. It's not for them. It's for the next group, and they pick it up. I picked up the dialogues of Plato when I was thirteen years old and started reading it, and I said, This is what I have been looking for. These are the conversations that I want to have, that I am starting to have and I haven't had. Or Edmond Rostand writes Cyrano and he dies and then these kids in the Bronx put on this play and I see it, and for me it's not the past . . . it's his past, it's Rostand's past, but it's my future. And so the work that I've done is my past, but it is somebody else's future, along with the thousands and thousands of other strands of literature that they will come upon and that helps humanity go forward.

17

DIANA SON

Photo by CYJO Photography

DIANA SON is an award-winning playwright, a writer and producer for television, and a screenwriter. Her plays *Stop Kiss* and *Satellites* premiered at The Public Theater. *Stop Kiss* won the GLAAD Media Award for Best New York Production and was on the Top 10 Plays lists of the *New York Times*, *New York Newsday*, the *New York Daily News*, and other major publications. Son also won the Berilla Kerr Award for playwriting. *Stop Kiss*, published as a trade paperback by Overlook Press, has been produced at hundreds of theatres nationally and abroad. Her play *BOY* premiered at La Jolla Playhouse under the direction of her frequent collaborator Michael Greif, and *Fishes* was produced by New Georges in New York City. Her short play *R.A.W. ('Cause I'm a Woman)* premiered at the Ohio Theatre in SoHo and has been anthologized in a number of collections.

Among the many theatres that have produced Son's plays are the Oregon Shakespeare Festival, Seattle Repertory Theatre, Woolly Mammoth Theatre Company, Delaware Theatre Company, Brava Theater Center, Geva Theatre Center, and People's Light and Theatre Company.

Son has been the recipient of an NEA/TCG Residency grant at the Mark Taper Forum and a Brooks Atkinson Fellowship at the Royal National Theatre in London. She has taught playwriting at Yale University and New York University and organized a playwriting workshop for caregivers of the disabled in Los Angeles, California.

Son was co-executive producer of the TV series *Law & Order: Criminal Intent* and has also written a number of TV pilots for CBS, a television movie for Showtime, and feature films for Fine Line and Robert Greenwald Productions. She is a member of the Writers Guild of America, East; the Dramatists Guild of America; and Women in Theatre; and is an alumnus of New Dramatists. She lives in Brooklyn, New York, with her husband.

I Will Follow

With love and supplication to J. D. Salinger for more than nine stories, *Hamlet* was to the sixteen-year-old me what *The Catcher in the Rye* was to everyone else in high school. Oh! I like the image that creates of teenage Diana. Literate. Possessed of gravitas and a black beret. But that picture would be a startling one to the dozen newly reunited "friends" of mine in the argot of Facebook. They would conjure a failed preppy. A second-stringer on the tennis team with a new wave haircut and the class slut for a best friend. I had several identities, but I never distinguished myself as particularly smart or serious. That was my older brother. (A history, science, and math whiz.) But thanks to a couple of gifted small-town public school teachers along the way, I learned to love books. The only class I looked forward to and did well in was English.

And oh, makers of fate, thank you, makers of fate, *thank you*, because in my senior year at Dover High School I got Phyllis Levitt as my Advanced Placement English teacher. Mrs. Levitt was in her forties at the time, had black and silver hair teased into a spider's tangle, and wore blue eyeshadow up to her eyebrows. A Brooklyn-raised Jew and New York University grad, I have no idea how she ended up in Dover, Delaware, where many of her students did farm chores before they came to school. But lucky for me she did and was a passionate and tough teacher who held our weekly Great Books class in her basement on Sunday nights. In our first month of the fall semester, she put *Hamlet* in our hands. And despite the alien quality of the iambic Elizabethan, Hamlet's character became accessible to me with his first lines. Hamlet is referred to as a university student, and as I was in the process of applying to colleges for the next year, I imagined him as eighteen. I recognized him as he answered his hypocritical stepfather's fake benevolence and concern with the timeless and timely language of teenagers, sarcasm.

When Claudius refers to Hamlet as both his nephew and his son—a crass acknowledgement of his shotgun wedding to his brother's widow—Hamlet responds that he's "A little more than kin, and less than kind." Claudius feigns nonchalance and asks why Hamlet is still so bummed out about his father's death. After all, it's been a full two months. Hamlet refers to Claudius' accusation that he is sulking under clouds with the riposte "Not so, my lord: I am too much i' the sun." I remember the thrill at realizing even a Danish prince from the 1600s would find it irresistible to sass a condescending parental figure.

In the next exchange, Hamlet's mother, Gertrude, speaks to him in a way that felt uncanny to me as the daughter of no-nonsense Korean immigrants. She is imperious and intolerant of his emotionality.

> Good Hamlet, cast thy nighted colour off,
> And let thine eye look like a friend on Denmark.
> Do not for ever with thy vailed lids
> Seek for thy noble father in the dust:
> Thou know'st 'tis common; all that lives must die,
> Passing through nature to eternity.

And I cheered when Hamlet, instead of being dismissed, tweaked Gertrude's words back at her. (Something I shamelessly did to my fluent but still English as a Second Language–speaking parents.) "Ay, madam, it is common."

And while Hamlet's brashness and ironic wit delighted me, it was ultimately his adolescent earnestness that made me love his character as if he were the brooding new boy in my sociology class. Nothing in my small-town teen life was even remotely analogous. But I empathized with Hamlet's struggle to take action when charged by his father with revenge.

We spent months reading and discussing *Hamlet*. One Sunday, Mrs. Levitt announced that she had seen an ad in the *New York Times* for an upcoming production of *Hamlet* at The Public Theater in New York City, directed by its founder, Joseph Papp. We all signed up for a field trip to go to New York and see it. We'd miss a whole day of school, and it portended to be more exciting than our other school field trips, which usually involved the Liberty Bell, DuPont Industries, or Joe Biden.

About a week before our trip, Mrs. Levitt made a sheepish confession. She'd just read a review of the production of *Hamlet* we were going to see and found out something she didn't know when she bought the tickets. "It's too late to exchange them, so we're just going to have to go," she said. My classmates and I groaned prophylactically. Most of us had never been to the theatre so we couldn't even imagine what this disturbing revelation would be. Mrs. Levitt continued, "Hamlet is being played by a woman. Diane Venora." Now I groaned with feeling. As much as it was an expression of disappointment, it was also the Foley effect of my brain being scrambled. How can Hamlet, who is so clearly a young man, be played by an actress? I pictured a woman with long blonde hair in a frilly dress lashing out, "Frailty, thy name is woman!" The only plays I'd ever seen were school plays and the Dover Community Singers' productions of *My Fair Lady* and *Fiddler on the Roof.* I had no concept of what gender-bender casting was, or even what an "interpretation" was. I assumed that when you went to the theatre you saw people in appropriate dress saying the lines from the play. I fully expected Hamlet to look like the guy on the cover of the Folger edition we were reading. I couldn't at all fathom how a woman could play a man.

We left Dover in a Greyhound bus around seven o'clock in the morning for the three-plus-hour drive to New York City. The mood on the bus was anticipatory despite the early hour. We were going to New York! Many of us had never been. My parents claimed to have taken me when I was little, but I had no memory of it—though their description of our ascent to Lady Liberty's crown, twenty-two stories high, evoked phantom leg cramps. What I was most excited about was checking out the used record stores I'd heard so much about. The closest venue any of the cool bands of the day would play was in Philadelphia, so my boyfriend and I would drive two hours to Philadelphia to see bands like U2, X, Gang of Four, Pretenders, and so on. We'd make a day of it and hit the record stores before the show. Historical note: before the Internet and iPods, used record stores were to indie music fans what eBay is to Trekkies. You could walk in and find the import-only 45 of XTC's "Senses Working Overtime" with the non-LP B-side, or the Japanese edition of U2's "Boy" with the alternate album cover—items far too esoteric for your local mall music store. Thumbing through the record bins itself was like sorting through treasure. It was a matter of what to choose amongst the riches. I'd heard through the grapevine that the best used record stores were in Greenwich Village, and I consoled myself that while *Hamlet* was going to suck, at least I'd get to score some amazing vinyl. The bus let us out outside The Public Theater, since that's where we'd board again at the end of the night. I remember stepping down onto the sidewalk and asking a passerby, "How do I get to Greenwich Village?" He threw up his hands and howled, "You're in it!" I spent the afternoon scouring Bleecker Bob's, Second Coming Records, Sounds at St. Marks . . . taking peripheral note of the purple NYU flags fluttering along my route from one record store to another. I bought a knish from a hot dog cart and went into carb rapture.

When I met back up with my classmates and Mrs. Levitt in the lobby of The Public Theater, I was in possession of a budget pirate's booty of imports and bootlegs, a Kate Bush T-shirt, and a white Pleather necktie bought from a street vendor. But my elation was quickly pierced. With its tall ceilings, chandeliers, and marble floors, The Public Theater lobby was the fanciest building I'd ever been in. And all the New Yorkers clustered in dark, magnetic mobs. I was immediately self-conscious. I felt as if I'd just parked my tractor

Pippa Pearthree as Ophelia and Diane Venora as Hamlet in the 1982 Public Theater production of Hamlet *at the Anspacher Theatre. (Photo © by Martha Swope, courtesy of the John Willis Theatre World/Screen World Archive)*

out front and walked in with muddy boots. Mrs. Levitt handed us our tickets, and we clambered up the stairs to the Anspacher Theater. Amongst the five theatres within The Public Theater complex, the Anspacher is the most history-evoking, particularly well suited for Shakespeare. It's a three-quarter space with two columns dividing the playing area. The seats are creaky squished red velvet and snap up when you lift your butt. I sat about fifteen rows back, house right—arms folded, feet digging into the floor. I was fighting my sense of being utterly out of my league culturally with a wariness of what kind of mayhem was going to be made out of my favorite play. When the actors came out I grudgingly allowed a thrill at how close they were, how clearly I could see their faces. Francisco and Bernardo, the guards keeping watch for Hamlet's father's ghost, welcome Horatio and Marcellus to their posts. Then Hamlet Sr.'s ghost came out and I found him, well, fake and kind of silly. I was used to movies where special effects made illusion believable.

For the next scene, the king, queen, and a whole court of characters (who's Cornelius? or Voltimand?) filed onto the stage. My eye was caught by a lithe, muscular figure leaning against a column, arms folded, his short, thick, dark hair falling just shy of his eyes. I had never heard the phrase "stage presence," but I was clearly responding to it. This actor was going to be interesting to watch. Since the play was going to suck, I decided I'd just keep my eye on this guy, even though he probably had a small role. I knew he wasn't Laertes, that macho goody two-shoes. It's a testament to my naiveté coupled disastrously with my insecurity that I couldn't deduce that the charismatic guy with the attitude was Hamlet. And then he spoke Hamlet's first lines which I knew so well, in an unforced alto. "Not so, my lord. I am too much i' the sun." Things moved slowly for me from that point on. I was suspended in a state of confusion. It was only after Hamlet finished his "Frailty, thy name is woman" speech that I thought to reach under my seat and rifle through my program, half expecting it to say that the ill-conceived casting of Hamlet by a woman had been corrected and that the role of Hamlet was now being played by (insert name of male actor). Instead, the Playbill stated without fanfare "Diane Venora *(Hamlet)*". I looked back at the stage. Hamlet was heartily greeting Horatio. And I slowly began to take it in—a woman was playing Hamlet *as a man*. I didn't know you could do that. And I finally absorbed that the point of casting a woman was not to desecrate the story. On the contrary, Venora's Hamlet was more faithful to my personal and passionate investment in Hamlet as an adolescent than the iconic performances imprinted by Olivier, John Gielgud, and Kevin Kline, who were all in middle age. Venora was thirty-one at the time, but with her open, easy-to-read face and compact body, she looked very much like a boy on the precipitous edge of manhood. Her portrayal of Hamlet was of a tortured teen, mercurial, explosive, desperate, and dysphoric. I was rapt. Seeing Hamlet as a young man but knowing, as if it were a secret, that he was being played by a woman (and I was a girl teetering at that precipice) engaged me viscerally. My first experience at the theatre was one in which I wasn't admiring good performances, visuals, and writing from a distance. I was being worked on alchemically. When the lights came up and the actors took their bows, I had the sinking realization that soon I would be on a Greyhound bus on the way back to Dover, Delaware, where there was no theatre. I had no idea when I would get the chance to see another play. And I knew I had to find my way back to the alchemist's lab. As our bus lumbered down lower Broadway, I took second note of the purple flags with the three letters on them. NYU.

I was still in the process of applying to colleges—with the intention of majoring in English and minoring in journalism. I requested the NYU course catalog and was stunned to find that there was a Department of Dramatic Literature and Theatre History that offered dozens of classes in which students read and examined plays. My eyes kept scanning one particular class, Drama in Performance in New York. I couldn't believe that there was a college where you could take a class whose purpose was to make you see theatre.

Mrs. Levitt was the first person I told outside of my family that I'd been accepted to NYU. I signed up for the Drama in Performance in New York class, but the first show I saw as a freshman was Anne Bogart's seminal revisionist production of *South Pacific* at NYU's Experimental Theatre Wing. Bogart set the musical in a mental institution for war veterans. The patients were performing *South Pacific*—and were being observed by doctors and nurses—as a way of reintegrating them into society. In a year, I went from being a total theatregoing neophyte to one who saw almost exclusively gender-bending, iconoclastic productions. I stayed in New York after graduating, waitressing, teaching English as a Second Language, and temping so that I could dedicate most of the day writing plays. After a few years of making the rounds on the short play circuit, I was invited into an Emerging Playwrights Lab at The Public Theater. We were encouraged to come during the day and write in one of the empty theatres if we wanted to. I was tempted—but demurred. Though I had been back to the Anspacher to see plays, I wasn't ready to present myself to it as a playwright. In 1998 my play *Stop Kiss* premiered at The Public Theater under the artistic directorship of George C. Wolfe, and my subsequent play, *Satellites*, debuted there during Oskar Eustis' inaugural season as artistic director. Currently working on my third play commission from The Public, I consider the place where I saw *Hamlet* my playwriting home. While in rehearsals for *Stop Kiss* I finally went back to the Anspacher and sat in the general area where I saw Joseph Papp's production twenty-six years ago. It wasn't just the play that changed my life. It was the play that gave me one.

18

REGINA TAYLOR

REGINA TAYLOR's credits as a playwright include *Oo-Bla-Dee*, for which she won the Mimi Steinberg/American Theatre Critics' Association New Play Award, *Drowning Crow* (her adaptation of Chekhov's *The Seagull*, which was produced on Broadway by Manhattan Theatre Club in its inaugural season at the Biltmore Theater and starred Alfre Woodard), *The Dreams of Sarah Breedlove*, *A Night in Tunisia*, *Escape from Paradise*, *Watermelon Rinds*, and *Inside the Belly of the Beast*. Taylor's critically acclaimed *Crowns* was the most frequently performed musical in the country in 2006. It is the winner of four Helen Hayes Awards, including one for Best Regional Musical. Taylor's latest play, *Magnolia*, premiered at Chicago's Goodman Theatre in March 2009. Taylor is a member and artistic associate of the Goodman Theatre.

Taylor is also an accomplished actress, best-known to television audiences for her role as Lilly Harper in the series *I'll Fly Away*. She received many accolades for her performance in the show, including a Golden Globe for Best Performance by an Actress in a Television Series, an NAACP Image Award for Outstanding Lead Actress in a Drama Series, and two Emmy Award nominations for Outstanding Lead Actress in a Drama Series. For Taylor's role of Molly Blane on the CBS hit drama *The Unit*, created by David Mamet and Sean Ryan, she took home the NAACP Image Award for Outstanding Actress in a Drama. Taylor has also starred in several blockbuster films, including *The Negotiator*, *Courage Under Fire*, *A Family Thing*, *The Keeper*, *Clockers*, *Losing Isaiah*, and *Lean on Me*. In addition to her film and television work, Taylor holds the honor as being the first Black woman to play Juliet in a Broadway production of Shakespeare's *Romeo and Juliet*. Her other Broadway credits include *As You Like It* and *Macbeth*. Her Off-Broadway credits include *Machinal*, *A Map of the World*, *The Illusion*, and *Jar the Floor*.

Adrienne Kennedy

Thomas: First time I heard Miles—He plays his first note and you know who he is—who you're talking to—who you're dealing with—just from his first breath. People *respect* him for that. That he found a sound that belongs only to him. All of them young ones—Coltrane—all of them study up under him—'cause he's found that—what every man wants: To own his own. But few dare.

Regina Taylor, *Magnolia*

No one writes like Adrienne Kennedy. Just as you recognize Miles Davis by the ear, Kennedy has one of the most unique voices of the American stage. She found that voice in writing her debut play *Funnyhouse of a Negro* upon taking a first trip to Africa. In her forty-year sojourn as a writer she explores the psyche of African American protagonists whose war with self overturns perspectives of race, gender, identity, history, and place in America.

Hers is a singular voice—outside of the singular voices of her contemporaries. Outside the naturalistic style of Lorraine Hansberry's *A Raisin in the Sun*, neither does she fit in with the social politics of Amiri Baraka or the Absurdist sensibility of Edward Albee, Kennedy's innovative style has always placed her on the outside of the outside. She has created plays that are complex, deeply confessional, surrealistic, and proudly contradictory starting with *Funnyhouse of a Negro*.

I landed outside The Public Theater in 1995 after seeing Signature Theatre Company's production of *Funnyhouse of a Negro*, directed by Carolyn Jackson Smith—feeling haunted, angered, saddened, and cathartic, wondering how I arrived at this moment outside the theatre on Lafayette Street, suppressing a primal need to yowl. And wondering how could I find the proximity of her depth in my own writing. I had read her plays along with Kennedy's *People Who Led to My Plays*, which is a wonderful companion guide to her journeys.

A recent book, *Understanding Adrienne Kennedy* by Philip C. Kolin, illuminates the pathways to Kennedy's body of work, taking us to the roots of her mythology through "her family and cultural background, her politics, and even her dreams." The book gives a map to Kennedy's hallucinatory works, howling trips through the American dream turned nightmare.

Though I loved reading her plays—it wasn't until I sat in the theatre that night and experienced her play *Funnyhouse* live—that I fully appreciated this most eviscerating, visceral, and experiential writer.

"You don't think of yourself as a great writer as you're pushing your shopping cart through D'Agostino's," Kennedy stated wryly in a conversation I had with her a few years back.* Then eighty-four, her voice—small and fragile but very resilient. Kennedy grew up a middle-class Negro child in Cleveland, Ohio, in a neighborhood of immigrants in the '30s and '40s. Each summer the family road in the "Coloreds Only" section of the train into Jim Crow–segregated Montezuma, Georgia, to visit their colored grandma, uncles, and aunts. While there Kennedy also visited the White neighborhood, where her mother's White father lived.

Kennedy's mother, Etta Hagabrook, was a light-skinned Black woman. Her dark-skinned father was a social worker. Both card-carrying members of the NAACP. Her father, who was very vocal against racial inequality, sounded like Martin Luther King to young Adrienne.

In school Adrienne excelled in the classics and Latin. She loved Virgil. Van Gogh, Bette Davis, Lena Horne. Light-skinned young Adrienne always kept her hair pressed straight and was taught to never speak what was on her mind but to always say what was "correct."

She began writing as a child. "Scribbling what my parents said. Their entire conversations. Scribbling alone in my room. . ."

"I was trying to imitate my mother when I started writing. She always told me her stories." Her mother's stories both funny and sad were anecdotes of the occurrences in her day, reminiscences about her past and her dreams. Her parents' stories would become the fabric of Kennedy's plays.

After graduating from Ohio State University (where Blacks were not allowed to major in English) with a degree in elementary education, Kennedy married Joseph Kennedy. After his return from Korea he worked on his Ph.D. at Columbia University in New York City, where Kennedy took writing classes.

"I couldn't get my work published. Twenty years of doing it. I felt I had failed. Two-and-a-half novels yet I couldn't get anything published."

In her twenties Kennedy was imitating Lorca, Tennessee Williams, Pushkin. "If I could just add more Charlotte Brontë . . . I had pent-up paragraphs and constantly being unhappy with what came out."

---

*Quotations, unless otherwise notated, are from the author's personal conversations with Adrienne Kennedy.

At the age of twenty-nine Kennedy took a trip with her husband to West Africa. "I got on that oceanliner, the *Queen Mary*. I was writing as soon as I got on that ship. It all seemed to take focus."

Kennedy and her husband traveled through Ghana and Nigeria. She was proud of letting her hair "go back" for the first time to its kinky roots. A transformation was happening deeper still. A discovery of her other selves. A change in how she saw herself and her work.

On that boat trip, between continents America and Africa, she embraced her past, her history, digesting the language of the Western writers, synthesizing the structures of African Theater, its mask work, transformative rituals, incantatory language, and surrealistic style.

She had a completed play when they sailed back home on the USS *United States*. That play—*Funnyhouse of a Negro*, directed by Michael Kahn and produced by Theatre 1964 (which consisted of Richard Barr, Clinton Wilder, and Edward Albee)—premiered in 1964. Billie Allen (the director of the most recent production of *Funnyhouse* at the Classical Theater of Harlem) was the play's heroine, the Negro-Sarah.

In Kennedy's newfound voice there is nothing "correct." *Understanding Adrienne Kennedy* points out that "Kennedy's play grew out of the turbulent early 1960s with its bloodshed over civil rights, the assassination of President John F. Kennedy in 1963, the Watts Riots in Los Angeles in 1965, and the looming holocaust of the Vietnam War. *Funnyhouse of a Negro* testified to an American culture of violence. Like Albee, Kennedy bravely brought taboo subjects into the theatre. *Funnyhouse of a Negro* explored incest, miscegenation, racial genocide, and female oppression years before they would be freely staged elsewhere."

Kennedy was also the first playwright to represent the self in multiple characters: "The Negro-Sarah is an Alice Through the Looking Glass, who sees herself in the distorted mirror of a Nightmare America where Black is evil. She is a colored girl who dreams of being White and commits suicide." She writes this years before Ntozake Shange's revelatory *for colored girls who have considered suicide when the rainbow is enuf.* Ntozake's play embraces this Sarah and all the little colored girls who have been on the edge of their existence; Ntozake reveals a pathway of redemption through their own eyes.

Kennedy's Sarah has only funhouse mirrors, reflecting a distorted and fractured since of self that leads her way off course.

With Sarah, Kennedy has created a character who—if my Grandma had witnessed her, she would have wagged her head and tsked, "That poor child."

Left to right: Ellen Bethea as Negro-Sarah, Caroline Clay as Queen Victoria Regina, and Lisa Renee Pitts as Duchess of Hapsburg in the 1995 Signature Theatre Company production of Adrienne Kennedy's Funnyhouse of a Negro. *(Photo © 1995 Susan Johann)*

In the same way she tsked and wagged during our yearly ritual of watching the tragic mulatto Pinkie in the movie *Imitation of Life*. Pinkie also tries to outrun her Blackness, only to come to self-realization tragically late—at her poor mother's funeral.

We see Sarah always in the same New York room that becomes other rooms from London to Africa. The room, lined with funhouse mirrors, are all in her mind. She is surrounded by her fractured selves that represent male/female, colonialists/colonized, Black/White, savior/denouncer. Her selves, divided into four parts—Queen Victoria Regina, the Duchess of Hapsburg (played by Black actors in whiteface/wannabe Whites, the darkest of the darkest martyred savior of the race), Patrice Lumumba, and Jesus (a distorted yellow dwarf)—all fight each other and take turns mocking Sarah. Attracted to and rebuffed by all sides, Sarah can't put the pieces of the mirror together; she fears recognizing herself. Confused and rootless, Sarah and all the characters are losing their hair, signifiers of their race. *Funnyhouse* is filled with dark wit and rage as this chorus of voices takes over her mind and tongue. Sarah loses her head and hangs herself.

In her late twenties, Kennedy confesses, "I was fearful of what I wrote. And then I would rewrite it and rewrite it until I didn't feel that fear anymore. I'd leave it alone. I'd look at it. "Who is that person!" They do make me feel intense emotions." She says she learned to leave the play in that place "where I feel uncomfortable. I learned not to censor."

The *Funnyhouse of a Negro* Sarah is the first in a line of Sarahs in Kennedy's plays. The earlier protagonists are killed off or go mad. Following *The Owl Answers*, the central character goes on and weathers the events to reappear in the next ritual. There is growth each time for each Sarah, through *She Talks to Beethoven* and *The Ohio State Murders*—through *Sleep Deprivation Chamber* and *Motherhood 2000*. They are resilient survivors. Kennedy's canon of work resonates as the lone and often arduous sojourn of the artist searching for self by way of her own unmistakable sound. A singular sound that cannot be denied or stifled. Through her work Kennedy has discovered that sound and created her own continent and language, which I entered into on that night at The Public.

Viewing this first Sarah in *Funnyhouse* was to view a soul laid bare—an autopsy, with all the biting humor and pain on display, guts and all spilling out on the stage—I wanted to look away but couldn't look away as all the ugly gray matter, usually hidden, oozed through the burrowed holes in her skull. And though I didn't want to recognize her—even though I wanted to distance myself—her humanity was inescapable. And even when I wanted to embrace her, her bones jutted out like sharp razors. And even when sudden hiccups of laughter of recognition escaped my clenched throat at the same time a growl of pain would displace my stomach. And I'm thinking—this is what it's like to write outside the margins . . . free.

This is what it's like to own one's own voice.

Paul: *To dare* to own your own sound.—Yeah.

Thomas: Yes. How he arrived at that—is a sweet mystery.

Regina Taylor, *Magnolia*

19

DOUG WRIGHT

In 2004 DOUG WRIGHT was awarded the Pulitzer Prize, a Tony Award, the Drama Desk Award, a GLAAD Media Award, an Outer Critics Circle Award, a Drama League Award, and a Lucille Lortel Award for his play *I Am My Own Wife*. In 2006 he received Tony and Drama Desk nominations for his book for the musical *Grey Gardens*. He wrote the book for the Broadway musical *The Little Mermaid*.

Wright won an Obie Award and the Kesselring Prize for Best New American Play from the National Arts Club for his play *Quills*. He went on to write the screenplay adaptation. The film was named Best Picture by the National Board of Review and nominated for three Academy Awards. His screenplay was nominated for a Golden Globe Award and received the Paul Selvin Award from the Writers Guild of America.

For the director Rob Marshall, Doug penned the television special *Tony Bennett: An American Classic*, which received seven Emmy Awards.

His plays have been produced across the United States and abroad, in countries as diverse as Romania, Australia, Zimbabwe, and Venezuela. Titles include *The Stonewater Rapture*, *Interrogating the Nude*, *Watbanaland*, *Buzzsaw Berkeley*, and *Unwrap Your Candy*.

Wright was recently honored with an award from the American Academy of Arts and Letters and the Tolerance Prize from the KulturForum Europa. He is a member of the Writers Guild of America, the Screen Actors Guild, the Society of Stage Directors and Choreographers, and the PEN American Center, which supports dissident writers across the globe. Wright's directing credits include *Kiki and Herb* in Washington, D.C., Philadelphia, and London. Acting credits include the films *Little Manhattan* and *Two Lovers*. Currently Wright serves on the board of the New York Theatre Workshop and is secretary of the Dramatists Guild. He lives in New York with his partner, the singer and songwriter David Clement.

Bruce and Charles

For most of my childhood, I was in love with my best friend, Bruce.

Bruce was a tall, blond Texan with the windswept good looks of a billboard model, and sometimes I would stare at him when he wasn't looking, just to memorize his face, with its slight Modigliani slant, the dash of asymmetry that saved him from Ken-doll perfection and instead gave him a slight perpetual scowl, the kind that catapulted him into the ranks of almost intolerable beauty, alongside James Dean and the rebel heroes of the French new wave.

My mother was always gracious to my friends, but she viewed Bruce with suspicion. Maybe it was the way he squealed past our house in his purple Chevy Monza, or his innate contempt for authority. Maybe he was just too pretty for a boy. Conversely, Mrs. C. used to warn Bruce against me. "Doug doesn't play a team sport," she'd say ominously, "and he spends all his time with that theatre crowd." Was I corrupting him, or was he corrupting me? It didn't matter. Either way, our mothers' shared belief that we were exerting an unwholesome influence over one another bonded us together with the force of Super Glue.

But Bruce did more than frighten my mother and set my adolescent pulse racing. He was my arbiter in the world of All Things New and Fabulous.

In 1979 Bruce rang me during dinner and said, "You've got to come over right away. I'm listening to this bootleg record, this new singer, she's amazing, and she's going to totally upset all the Catholics because she calls herself Madonna. Can you believe that? *Madonna?*"

Another time he summoned me to his house because he had—in his words—"redecorated his room." When I arrived, he opened his bedroom door with the same hushed reverence a monk might show when unlatching the gate to the reliquary at Sacré Coeur. Hanging from the ceiling were thirty or forty plastic dishracks, bolted upside down, and filled with brightly colored disposable plates, saucers, and cups, which he'd placed in the oven just long enough to melt ever so slightly; they dangled over us like so many Tupperware stalactites. I looked at him, dumbstruck. "Pop art," he whispered softly.

In high school Bruce became my first director. For drama class we decided to make our own film, using his father's Brownie camera. The story we chose was universal: a first date. A randy boy would make unseemly moves on a hapless virgin. But the shocking *coup de théâtre*? I'd play both roles! As the predatory teen, I wore knickers with a varsity sweater and a jaunty cap perched sideways on my head. For the girl, we raided his sister's Halloween closet and found a gingham dress and a blond wig with corkscrew ringlets. Through the miracle of editing (which in those days was accomplished with some tape and a razor blade), I would appear to be seducing myself! When the film debuted at McCulloch Middle School to a room filled with seventh graders, it was a rousing success.

It was in college that Bruce granted me another seminal first. I was struggling to come out of the closet, and Bruce paid me an all-important visit during spring break. He'd proudly proclaimed himself gay years before, and I urgently needed his help. "I've told everyone I'm gay," I blurted to him. "My family, my friends . . . but it doesn't make me feel any better."

"Why not?" he asked.

"Because it's a wholly academic admission," I told him. "I don't have any experience to confirm it. I've never . . ."—my heart stopped beating but my mouth kept moving—". . . *had sex with a man.*"

A sly smile crept over his face. "Well," he said, clicking off the light, "Let's take care of that, shall we?"

....

That was the first and only time we slept together. On one level, I was devastated that we never became lovers. But on another level, I took it in stride. Our relationship was long and complicated, but our roles had become concretized over the years: he was the Golden Boy, the A-list gay, who matched the lifestyle spreads in *After Dark* magazine. I was his bookish best friend, the neurotic artist, homely but consoled by my pretensions of intellect and talent. He gave me beauty; I gave him gravitas. We exchanged attributes in lieu of bodily fluids; it was our unspoken pact. And both of us were far too comfortable inhabiting those tropes to risk disaster and fashion new ones.

Bruce and I went to college in different states and missed one another fiercely, so we agreed not to repeat that mistake in graduate school. I'd study theatre at the Tisch School of the Arts, and he'd head uptown to Columbia for a medical degree. Together, we'd conquer New York, plumbing its hidden corners, insinuating ourselves into its demimonde.

One night Bruce announced, "I've got theatre tickets. There's this troupe near Sheridan Square that we just *have* to see."

"How did you hear about them?" I asked.

"Kip the towel boy," Bruce answered, confirming that his late-night social contacts far exceeded my own. "He says they're the last authentic thing left in the West Village."

From the outside, the theatre didn't look like much—little more than a storefront with cheap wooden letters that spelled out RIDICULOUS THEATRICAL COMPANY. Lingering near the door, goths, gay couples with matching muttonchops, leftist neighborhood types with gray ponytails and fringe, and a few befuddled tourists who'd been lured downtown by half-price coupons. Inside there was a cramped vestibule and a tiny ticket window with bars; rather than a real person, I half-expected to find an automated gypsy with a coin-drop crystal ball.

After we picked up our tickets, an usher gestured to a staircase that spiraled down into the basement. It was painted in an explosion of colors and led straight into the psychedelic lobby below. I felt like I'd strayed onto the back lot of an especially trippy Sid and Marty Krofft show. There were placards bearing reviews, most notably from the oracular *New York Times*.

"The company's been around for years," Bruce informed me. "Now they're on the dangerous brink of mainstream success."

We shuffled our way into the house; the ceilings were unusually low, and the seats looked like they'd been salvaged from a fire sale. The stage itself tilted toward the audience at a precarious angle, as though a single misstep could send an actor sliding into your lap. But the red curtain with gold fringe belied these humble surroundings; it harked back to an era when the theatre was the province of Kings.

The houselights dimmed; we heard a thunder crack, and the howling of the wolves across the moors. The play began.

....

The Mystery of Irma Vep billed itself as a penny dreadful. In it, newlywed Lady Enid arrives at Mandacrest, the English manor house of her husband Lord Edgar. She expects a life of bucolic splendor, but instead she falls headlong into a nightmare. Edgar's late wife, the titular Irma, still haunts the grounds, and she's none too happy that a new bride is attempting to usurp her place. Poor Lady Enid is mortified; what vengeful spirits has she unwittingly bestirred? For solace, she turns to the housemaid Jane. But Jane is a surly old crow reminiscent of Mrs. Danvers in Hitchcock's *Rebecca*, unable to comfort Enid because of the twisted love she still bears for her dead mistress. Meanwhile, Nicodemus, the butler, stomps about the chilly old house on a wooden leg—a replacement for one lost during an unfortunate interlude with a werewolf—spouting ill omens and tales of a murdered child. When Lady Enid attempts to unlock the many secrets of Mandacrest, she learns that even Lord Edgar is not who he seems. Is he willfully attempting to drive his second wife mad? (Cue the organ music!) Before it all comes to a suitably blood-soaked conclusion, our heroine has fought off wild dogs, exposed vampires, and even detoured as far away as Egypt to conceal herself inside a fourteenth-century sarcophagus. (Don't ask.) The play's influences were many: Daphne du Maurier, Matthew "The Monk" Lewis, Hammer Film Productions, and the French Grand Guignol. Careening from arch drawing-room comedy to Vincent Price horror flick, the writing navigated genres with the same deceptive ease as a ship's captain navigating the high seas.

The stagecraft was simple but ingenious: the set was peppered with trap doors, hidden mirrors, and surprise passageways. But the show's chief, virtuosic pleasure? Two actors played all the parts. One happened to be the playwright himself, Charles Ludlam. In a wig and plunging neckline (revealing his hirsute décolletage), his Lady Enid swept onto the stage with all the authority of Lynn Fontanne. As Nicodemus, he'd lurch across the stage in his prosthetic, comic wisps of hair dancing over an otherwise bald scalp, his eyes as wide and incredulous as a lemur's. He articulated each character with hilarious precision by elevating his voice an octave or screwing his rubber face into a wholly new profile. (I blushed to recall that I attempted the same trick once, in humbler circumstances, in front of Bruce's camera. Now I was getting a master class.)

Even in my youth, I knew Ludlam was that rare, indispensable creature: a bona fide clown. Not of the cloying, circus variety, no, but a clown in the tradition of Bert Lahr or Charlie Chaplin, consummate artists who can make us laugh uproariously at our own foibles and in the same instant break our hearts.

Ludlam's partner in crime (and later, I would learn, his longtime lover) was Everett Quinton. He not only kept pace with his formidable costar, he'd designed all the costumes, too. He'd exit stage right as Lord Edgar in his morning coat and cravat, only to reenter stage left as Jane in her immaculate apron and maid's cap. Mr. Quinton was a master not only of comic timing, but of Velcro.

Along with the rest of the audience, Bruce and I laughed until our ribs ached; but our reaction was more profound then mere amusement. For the first time in our lives, we felt truly *at home*.

Maybe it was the hilariously two-dimensional set; hand painted with its many booby traps, it didn't look so dissimilar from the flats Bruce and I had painted back in Texas for the senior play. Maybe it was the gleeful, unabashed cross-dressing. Maybe it was the coded gay references that glittered in the text like so many hidden jewels. Whatever it was that made us feel such acute belonging, we knew one thing: when the curtain call ended, we couldn't bear the thought of going. Leaving the theatre after a peak experience is always a wistful affair; but we sat in our seats for a long time, too smitten to even stand.

....

After that fateful evening, Bruce and I became scholars of the Ridiculous. We read up on the company's early work, far more outré than even the outrageous *Irma Vep*—plays with delicious, profane titles like *Turds in Hell* and *Isle of Hermaphrodites*. We found photos of other company members: John Vaccaro, the secondhand book merchant and tempestuous director who'd originally founded the group; winsome leading lady Black-Eyed Susan; and the sexually ambiguous Mario Montez, star of the Jack Smith film *Flaming Creatures*. We vowed to descend that kaleidoscopic staircase again and again, to keep abreast of the company's future work.

Soon we had an established ritual. We'd meet at the Monster, a gay bar in Sheridan Square known for its cheerful seediness and show-tune sing-alongs. A quick drink, and at curtain time, we'd cross the street. After the play, we'd grab a late supper, usually at a coffee shop, and discuss the play over greasy fries in a vinyl banquette.

"There was an announcement in the *Voice*," Bruce told me one evening, dabbing the ketchup from his chin. "Next up at the Ridiculous? An adaptation of Flaubert's novel *Salammbô*."

"Have you read it?" I asked.

"No," said Bruce, "But *get this*." He arched an eyebrow and leaned over the table, lowering his voice to a confidential tone. "The production features live doves, six naked bodybuilders, and a five-hundred-pound actress, totally nude, covered in prosthetic scars to simulate the last, fatal stages of leprosy."

What further enticement did we need?

We bought our tickets early to three performances over the course of the show's run. The reviews for *Salammbô* were as savage as the notices for *Irma Vep* had been ecstatic. But in our dark little hearts, we preferred it. It had a decadence, an unapologetic extravagance, that spoke to us as young gay men who were both exhilarated and terrified by our own outsider status in the larger culture.

Bruce became infatuated with one particular actor in *Salammbô*. His name was Philip Campanaro, and he played Matho the Barbarian. Mr. Campanaro's negligible acting skills and thick Noo Yawk accent were mitigated by a chiseled Italian face and the body of a veritable Tarzan. He performed his role in a loincloth seemingly made of kite string, and his only previous show-business experience had been a pictorial in a magazine with the evocative title *Torso*. He wooed the heroine (Ludlam, of course) with lines like "Come to me, I love thee more than life, virgin who meltest my soul." Onstage, Salammbô swooned. In row F, three seats off the aisle, so did Bruce.

A few months later my telephone rang.

"Guess what?" Bruce exclaimed. "Philip Campanaro is starring in the next Ridiculous show. It's a send-up of James M. Cain film noirs called *The Artificial Jungle*. It's set in a pet shop. There's a piranha tank onstage, and a six-foot-tall drag queen who does back flips."

"We are *so* going," I said.

....

Bruce and I became acolytes too late.

When we first stumbled into his theatre, Ludlam had been penning scripts for over twenty years, beginning with *Big Hotel* in 1966. We had all the fervor and enthusiasm of fresh converts and imagined we'd continue to worship at Sheridan Square for the foreseeable future. So it was with considerable shock and dismay that we read in the May 20, 1987, edition of the *New York Times* that he had been hospitalized with double pneumonia. Like most gay men during those perilous years, we knew that the phrase "pneumonia" usually indicated something far graver. We'd barely come to know the work of Charles Ludlam. Was it already time to mourn him?

Cruelly, the virus began to overtake Ludlam when his creativity was at its absolute peak. He was opening in his first major Hollywood feature, a film called *The Big Easy*. He was slated to direct *Titus Andronicus* in Central Park, write a new play based on the life of magician Harry Houdini, and complete his long-awaited film *The Sorrows of Dolores*. In short, he was about to fully inhabit the life he'd been working years to earn.

In interviews he continued to promote his future projects, undaunted, barely acknowledging his illness. Perhaps he still hoped to create a lifetime's worth of art in the few weeks he had left. Who knows? Maybe he believed he could ward off death in a final blast of productivity. But none of his anticipated projects would move forward. Instead, at the age of only forty-four, Charles Ludlam died.

At the time, Bruce was living in a sixth-floor walk-up that happened to overlook Sheridan Square. He telephoned me from his window. "I can see the theatre," he said. "It's amazing. Fans are stopping by to leave flowers, cards, and gifts."

Instantly, in my heart, I knew I wanted to scrawl a few words on paper and leave them on the growing pile. But I was too embarrassed to say so. After all, I'd never even met Ludlam. I'd just been one in a legion of fans. It felt corny; presumptive, even. But with his usual intuition, Bruce read my mind.

"Why don't you come down and see for yourself?" he asked. Something in his voice made it sound like a request instead of an invitation.

I pulled on my shoes and walked down to his place. I trudged up the endless stairs. When he met me at the door, Bruce didn't look good. His face bore a distracted, washed-out look, like he'd taken the news of Ludlam's death with unusual severity. I asked him for a piece of stationery so I could compose a note. I can't remember its exact contents, but it went something like this:

> Dear Mr. Ludlam,
> When I heard your characters speak for the first time, I
> started to find my voice, too. Thank-you.
> D. W.

It was an unabashed, even corny sentiment, no doubt, but profoundly heartfelt all the same. I sealed the envelope.

"Do you want to come with me?" I asked Bruce.

"No," he told me. "You go ahead."

Outside, it was already muggy, and I could feel the Christopher Street subway roaring underneath my feet. I walked over to the theatre and slipped my card among the many that had been wedged beneath the security gate guarding the entrance. Before leaving, I glanced up to Bruce's window. I could see him in silhouette, pensive. I thought of waving but decided that I shouldn't. It felt vulgar, like I'd be interrupting his solitude.

A short time later, Bruce's worst fears were confirmed. He, too, was diagnosed with HIV.

....

Although I never met Ludlam, I would have the privilege of working with two estimable members of his company.

In 1989, the director Christopher Ashley, the composer Michael John LaChiusa, and I concocted a late-night spoof of horror movies called *Buzzsaw Berkeley*. At the time we thought it was a comic masterpiece of considerable subversive magnitude. In retrospect, it was strictly Ridiculous Theater Lite, without the breadth of literary reference or theatrical cunning. But it did have its pleasures, and chief among them was the star performance of Ethyl

Ethyl Eichelberger as Mrs. Nurdiger and Charles Ludlam as Chester Nurdiger in the 1986 Ridiculous Theatrical Company production of Charles Ludlam's The Artificial Jungle. *(Photo by Anita and Steve Shevett)*

Charles Ludlam (on floor) as Salammbo, Everett Quinton as Taanach, and Ethyl Eichelberger as Hamilcar Barca with members of the Company of the 1985 Ridiculous Theatrical Company production of Charles Ludlam's adaptation of Gustave Flaubert's novel Salammbo. *(Photo by Anita and Steve Shevett)*

Eichelberger, the aforementioned six-foot-tall drag queen who'd been featured in *The Artificial Jungle*.

Eichelberger was also an erstwhile wig and costume designer for the Ridiculous and a playwright, too; he had authored an abridged *Lear* in which he portrayed all the parts, as well as inventive retellings of *Medea* and *Hamlet*. Sometimes his work boasted the classical pedigree suggested by his training at the American Academy of Dramatic Art. At other times it was sheer burlesque. But each play usually afforded him the opportunity to show off his three most extravagant skills: playing the accordion, doing triple backflips, and eating fire.

In our show Ethyl played a fearless double role: in the first act he was an aging Ziegfeld showgirl, and in the second he was the demented choreographer Buzzsaw Berkeley, so named because as the result of a tragic industrial accident, he was forced to live with chainsaws in lieu of human arms.

I'll never forget one performance in particular. My parents had flown up from Dallas see the show. I hasten to add that they are lovely people, more progressive than our Texas provenance might suggest, but I was still nervous. In those days I was young and foolish enough to read my reviews, and the critics had been wildly mixed. But on one point they unanimously agreed: the show was gleefully crass, just begging to have its mouth washed out with soap. One paper had dubbed its humor "vulgarity times velocity," and John Simon, then of *New York* magazine, had proclaimed, "The gayest event in New York since the Stonewall Riots!" (Instead of feeling the sting he intended, we wanted to quote him on T-shirts.) But how on earth would my parents react?

During the first act I lurked nervously in the rear of the theatre, trying to assess their reaction. Regrettably, I couldn't see their faces. But my heart leapt into my throat when Ethyl (in full Ziegfeld drag, sequins, and a magnificent feathered headdress) stopped the show, cold, to announce, "Pardon me. I heard a rumor that the playwright's parents are here. Would you stand, please?" My mother and father obliged. Ethyl hiked up his skirt and descended from the stage in platform heels. He sauntered right down the center aisle of the theatre, and took my father's hand. "You must be Mr. Wright!" he exclaimed. My father turned a deep shade of pink. Ethyl inspected my dad's chair. "Oh my God," he bellowed. "He's been laughing so hard at his son's jokes, he's peed all over his seat!" Then he cued the pianist, and inquired of my father, "May I have this dance?"

Dad consented. Mother looked on. And I was incalculably moved. There was my father, his whole face broken open in a sheepish grin, while he did the rumba with a towering queen in a strawberry-blond fall. My mother watched, beaming. To me, the world had never before seemed like such a generous and loving place.

Before we left, my father insisted we pay a visit to the stage door so he could ask Ethyl to personally autograph his program.

....

In 1993 I wrote a one-act play that, like the musical that preceded it, owed an enormous debt to Ludlam and the Ridiculous. It featured baroque, overripe language, unapologetic perversity, and all manner of antique stagecraft: thunder sheets, lightning flashes, ventriloquism, and puppetry. Only this time, I'd found a subject large enough to be served by all these stylistic flourishes instead of upstaged by them: the Marquis de Sade. The title of the piece was *Quills*.

At the very first reading of the play at the New York Theater Workshop, I noticed a certain member of the audience. It was Lola Pashalinski, one of Ludlam's most celebrated leading ladies. Born Regina Hirsch in Brooklyn, she'd joined the company years before he did, when it was under the stewardship of John Vaccaro. She'd originated the roles of Lola Lola in *Corn* and Miss Cubbish in *Bluebeard*. I was enormously flattered that she'd thought to attend my humble reading. As the actors leapt into the text, I became immediately self-conscious. "Surely," I thought, "she'll see right through my play. She'll divine Ludlam's influence in every speech, in every gesture." But another thought followed on the heels of that one: "Why is she in the audience? Doesn't she belong onstage, with the rest of my cast?"

Then and there, I decided to enlarge the play, make it two acts, and create a role especially for Lola: the Marquis' wife, Renée Pelagie, forever martyred by her husband's libidinous indiscretions. Much to my delight, Lola consented to play it.

Rehearsals were not always smooth sailing. One day Lola became highly agitated. "This role is a departure for me," she murmured, discontent. "I've got to push beyond my customary bag of tricks." Inside, I panicked. Clearly, she regarded her flamboyant clowning with the Ridiculous as too frivolous for the role of Renée. But inside, I screamed, "Lola! This role is written for those very tricks! It's been lovingly crafted in that very same tradition!"

Still, she surprised me. She didn't abandon her years of Ridiculous training; she landed every preposterous joke with flair and created a bristling physicality for her character, which rivaled such camp icons as Marie Dressler and Marjorie Main. But like her one-time mentor, she catapulted the role beyond mere parody. She gave Renée a truly tortured soul; beneath her comic exterior, there was the very darkest kind of pain, an agony that befitted the woman married to history's most notorious sadist. It was a star performance.

....

Quills was widely reviewed by the New York press when it opened at the New York Theater Workshop in 1995, but to my astonishment, not one critic cited its obvious debt to Ludlam. Yet his name would come up in relation to the play five years later, under very different circumstances.

I was in London at Pinewood Studios, where we were shooting my screen adaptation. The marvelous Australian actor Geoffrey Rush had been cast as the Divine Marquis, and he employed a variety of colorful means to access the role. First and foremost, he liberally doused himself with patchouli oil, which he felt epitomized the character's playboy decadence. He'd been poring through Sade's writing, as well, and done due diligence with the multitudinous academic tomes about his life. Still, he confided to me, he'd yet to nail the precise tone for the role.

Then it happened. One morning, I felt him grab me by the arm while I was helping myself to a quintessentially British cheese-and-chive sandwich at the Craft Services table. I turned to see him in full Sadean regalia: the gray wig, curled like two ram's horns, his white brocade jacket, and his silken breeches with pointed shoes. "It's Ludlam, isn't it?" he whispered to me fervently. "I reread the play last night. It's pure Theatre of the Ridiculous!"

A grin broke over my face like the dawn. Of course he knew Ludlam! Despite his status as the most coveted character actor in Hollywood, Geoffrey was first and foremost a man of the theatre.

"This role," he continued, licking his lips in gleeful discovery, "hovers deliriously between King Lear and Norma Desmond." He could've been describing a performance by Ludlam himself.

The film earned Geoffrey his third Academy Award nomination.

....

After Ludlam's death, his lover Everett Quinton took over the reins of the Ridiculous. Bruce and I continued to attend faithfully. We saw a posthumous production of Ludlam's last script, *How to Write a Play*, and revivals of seminal favorites like *Camille* and *Eunuchs of the Forbidden City*. We even saw a new play, *Brother Truckers*, penned by one of Ludlam's most compelling protégés, a strapping young playwright named Georg Ostermann. It had all the hallmarks of the Master's works: a giddy, preposterous plot, wigs as high as wedding cakes, and a fortifying perversity in the face of Manhattan's Banana Republic banality. For a time, it looked as if the theatre might bloom anew.

But despite Quinton's heroic efforts, the playhouse struggled without its Svengali. Audiences dwindled. Uncharitably, the landlord jacked up the rent. Worse still, other key company members fell prey to the burgeoning plague. Ethyl Eichelberger took his own life, with a razor in the bathtub, because his fragile body couldn't tolerate his HIV medication. Not long after his triumph, the bright young phoenix Georg Ostermann was hospitalized, only to die a few weeks later.

"I went by the Ridiculous today," Bruce offered idly one night over cosmos. "They've taken the sign down and bolted the door. Someone plastered up a sign; says they've closed, once and for all."

In the idiosyncratic world of New York real estate, the building sat empty for what seemed like forever. I'd pass it on my frequent walks through the village. The sight of it, abandoned and forlorn, gave me sharp pangs in my stomach. I'd look at it and think, "Pandora's Box, sealed shut again."

....

Bruce was fortunate, I suppose. Despite the damning nature of the diagnosis in those days, he still had a few good years left. During them, he successfully completed his M.D. in psychiatry and fell in love. Unsurprisingly, perhaps, his new lover bore the swarthy good looks of his Ridiculous crush, Philip Campanaro, but with impeccable diction and a business degree from Wharton besides.

With his new flame, Bruce set up house in a trendy apartment building in the Village, near the West Side Highway. He adored it, because it was sleek and fashionable but he could still hear the trannie hookers in the meatpacking district outside his window, haggling with their johns. "It keeps me humble," he'd say, "and so entertained."

But the virus proved to be as malicious to Bruce as it had been to Charles Ludlam. Just when all the pieces of his life had clicked firmly into place—the house, the spouse and med school graduation—a host of infections took hold. Some days he could barely walk. Within a month or two he could no longer eat and was forced to adopt a feeding tube. His vanity took the cruelest hit of all. The medications gave his face a sallow, bloated cast, and his lissome body began to atrophy.

We both knew the end was approaching with devastating swiftness. The thought of weathering the next fifty or sixty years without my best friend was inconceivable to me. "You haven't even gone yet," I'd tell him, "and I miss you already."

....

Scant weeks before he died, Bruce gave me an astonishing gift, as profound as the evening he'd first urged me to join him for a night of theatre on Sheridan Square. Like Ludlam in the waning days of his life, Bruce found solace in a crowning, maniacal surge of creativity.

"Can you come over?"

His voice on the telephone was weak, but his tone was insistent. I'd become accustomed to these calls. His lover frequently traveled on business, so Bruce was often alone. Sometimes he needed an emergency prescription. Other times he was having a rare craving, able to ingest food, and wanted a midnight Big Mac or a box of lemon cookies. Regardless, I'd drop everything and half-walk, half-run to his apartment.

I'll never forget stepping foot inside his place on that particular night. The air had a pungent, chemical smell like wet enamel. Inside, the stereo was pounding out the Pet Shop Boys. As I rounded the hallway, I could see a plastic tarp spread out across the living room floor.

Bruce lay, spent, on the couch, in a pair of boxer shorts and medical school scrubs speckled with paint. When he saw me, a vague smile flickered across his face. He nodded toward the wall.

An enormous canvas was leaning against it. It must've been five feet square. Against a base coat of industrial gray, there were exuberant, angry squiggles of Day-Glo color: lime greens and cerulean blues and Hello Kitty pinks. It was as antic as Jackson Pollock, and as lurid as LeRoy Neiman. It stood there, still glistening, like a crazy, neon road map for a trip Bruce would never take, ribbons of color, chaotic and free-form. I'd never seen anything quite like it except, perhaps, in the old lobby of the Ridiculous Theatrical Company.

"How on earth did you—" I started to say.

But the answer to my question was lying at his feet: curled tubes of acrylic paint, flattened and empty like old toothpaste. In a nearby wastebasket, there must have been fifty or sixty old syringes, the very ones Bruce had used to administer his drugs. He'd filled them with paint in lieu of meds and, in a mad dance, expunged them onto the canvas. It was a remarkable gesture, one that taunted fate, defiant and celebratory at a time when Bruce knew that he was losing everything.

"Take a look at the title," he encouraged me. "It's meant to be a portrait."

I glanced at the lower right hand corner of the painting. Slyly etched in thin, calligraphic script were the words "Essence of Doug." Bruce looked at me, triumphant and amused at the same time, eager to assess my reaction.

"It's a good likeness," I said.

"You're a complicated fellow," he teased me. "You've got a lot going on inside."

I grinned back at him, but my eyes were welling with tears. "What on earth are you going to do with it?" I asked him.

"Take it," he said in his deceptively casual tone. "It's yours."

Bruce died a few months later. Long after his funeral, for over a decade, the painting hung in my apartment.

....

My life is much changed now. I am married to a loving husband, handsome and funny, a songwriter and performer with talent enough for both of us. Soon David and I will celebrate our sixth anniversary. Our relationship is remarkably healthy, unmarred by unrequited desire. My plays, once born of postadolescent rage and disenfranchisement, have become notably kinder. If *Quills* was in some ways a scornful diatribe, then *I Am My Own Wife* is a love letter. I've even penned the book to a Disney musical, *The Little Mermaid*— one of the happiest experiences of my career.

Bruce's painting sits in a storage facility, wrapped in bubble wrap and boxed in a crate. I tell myself that I'll pull it out again when we've finally bought that elusive country house. Nearby, in a locked file cabinet, third drawer, are old programs from the last, fleeting glory days of the Ridiculous, yellow now with age. I can't throw them away. Someday, I have to believe, they'll have incalculable value to a theatre archive or university. For now, they sit patiently in the dark.

In my memory, Bruce and Charles are forever linked. They both taught me enduring lessons that I still carry close to my heart. Our greatest work is often forged at our most perilous moments. The written word, the painted image; these are the only means we have to refute death. And sometimes, the bravest art lies in the fearless realm of the extreme.

ACKNOWLEDGMENTS

The American Theatre Wing would like to acknowledge the significant contributions made by its board member William Craver, who was the original guide for this project and who fielded many queries regarding agent representation as well as providing valuable editorial input. The Wing also wishes to thank Patricia Crown of Coblence & Associates, who provided invaluable counsel on legal matters, and Bert Fink and Bill Rosenfield for their help on the book. The Wing staff should be acknowledged for their assistance on so many tasks connected with this project.

Editor Ben Hodges would like to extend his personal thanks to Bob Anderson; Epitacio Arganza; Raj Autencio; Ben Feldman Esq. and Beigelman, Feinter, and Feldman PC; Jed Bernstein and the Commercial Theater Institute; Jason Cicci; June Clark; Richard Cohen; Sue Cosson; Susan Cosson; Carol and Nick Dawson; Tim Deak; Scott Denny; Amanda Flynn; Gretchen, Aaron, Max, and Eli Kerr; Al and Sherry Hodges; Robert Levine; Katie Love; Andrew Kirtzman, Louis DelVechhio, and the Madison Fire Island Pines; Tony Meisel; Lucy Nathan; John Philip Esq.; Angie and Drew Powell; Carolyn, David, Glenna, and David Rapp; Rob Rokicki; Lesa Reed; Aaron Scharff; Wilson Valentin; Bill and Sarah Willis; George Wilson; and Shane Wolters.

Together, the American Theatre Wing and Ben Hodges would like to extend joint thanks to the many people who worked to make this book a reality. Particular thanks for the acquisition of this book go to Michael Messina, and for the subsequent stewardship and support of this project to John Cerullo, Carol Flannery, Clare Cerullo, Marybeth Keating, Diane Levinson, and Aaron Lefkove at Applause Theatre & Cinema Books and the Hal Leonard Corporation.

Jeremy Megraw, photographic librarian at the Billy Rose Theatre Division of the New York Library for the Performing Arts, has been a silent partner in helping assist in determining photographic rights holders, a core part of putting together a publication such as this.

Thanks go to contributing personal photographers Peter Sumner Walton Bellamy, Tom Bloom, Monique Carboni, Cindy Hwang/CYJO Photography, Stephanie Diani, Jon Robin Baitz, Scott Council, Colleen Dodson-

Baker, Brad Hampton, Ethan Hill and Getty Images, Kristin Hoebermann, Susan Johann, Joan Marcus, Walter McBride/Retna, Jennifer Reiley, Craig Schwartz, John Schisler, and Eric Williams for allowing us to reprint their notable playwrights' photos.

Thanks to production photographers and rights holders Marsha Hudson and the estate of Bert Andrews; Phyllis Curtin; Nilo Cruz; William and Madelyn Ganslen; Gerry Goodstein; Terry Koshel and the estate of Martha Holmes; Susan Johann; Werner Kuhn; Janet Johnson and Brigitte Lacombe; Michael Shulman at Magnum Photos; Ron Mandelbaum at Photofest; Kathleen Ruhl and the estate of Pat Ruhl; Carol Rosegg; Sheldon Secunda; Steve and Anita Shevett; Dave Siccardi; Reverend Trevor Nicholls, president of Cardinal Spellman High School in the Bronx, New York, as well as the Cardinal Spellman archdiocesan lawyer; John Stern; Martha Swope; and Alfredo Valente and Richard Valente, for allowing us to reprint and in some instances providing for us the photographs themselves. A special thank you to the John Willis Theatre World/Screen World Archive, which Ben Hodges manages, is owed the greatest permissions debt of all. It would simply not have been possible to produce this book without the permissions-free access to one of the most important archives of the twentieth-century American theatre that we have been given by Mr. Willis.

There would have been no publication at all had the representatives of the talent here assembled not allowed us access to them, and for that kudos go to agents and their assistants Ron Gwiazda, Peter Hagan, and Eric Stein at Abrams Artists; Alexis Williams and Bret Adams Ltd.; Scott Burkhardt; George Lane, Anna Benziger, Corinne Haroun, Naveen Kumar, Hannah Swihart, Tiffanye Threadcraft, Jason Cooper, Olivier Sultan, and Creative Artists Agency; Patrick Herold, Kenneth Ferrone, and International Creative Management; William Craver, Sadie Jones, and Paradigm Agency; Sarah Miles; Andrew Russell; Sarah Jane Leigh, Barbara Stansell, and Sterling Standard; Peregrine Whittlesey; Valerie Day, Jonathan Lomma, Peter Franklin, and William Morris Endeavor; Catrina Walsh; and Michelle Weilert.

No less important on numerous other matters of professional service are Evren Odcikin and American Conservatory Theater; Nicole Estavanik and *American Theatre* magazine; Leigh Nicholas and the Barbican Centre; Dr. Carey C. Newman and Baylor University Press; Ellen Carr of the College of Fine Arts at Boston University; Sharon Lehner, archivist, and the Brooklyn Academy of Music; Raymond Butti Jr. and the Brown University Archives; John Brown; Marion Castleberry; Uriah Leddy and City Theatre Company; Glenn Close; Richard Curry; Hallie Foote and the estate of Horton Foote, Amanda Flynn; Allison Rawlings and the Geffen Playhouse; Patricia O'Conner and grammarphobia.com; David Marshall Grant; Jonathan Groff, Pamela Madsen and Harvard Theatre Collection, Houghton Library, Harvard University; Jakob Holder; Bartlett Sher and Intiman Theatre; David Kaufman; Zachary Kleinsmith; Norman Levy; Erica Owens and La Jolla Playhouse; John Lithgow; Randy Ellen Lutterman; Caitlin Baird, Debra Waxman, and Manhattan Theatre Club; Todd London and New Dramatists; Dawn Buck and New Stage Theatre of Jackson, Mississippi; Michael Hopkins and PARS International; Patty Onagan and Pasadena Playhouse; Hal Prince, Jesse Alick, Sam Neuman, and The Public Theater; Everett Quinton; Lynn Redgrave; Helen Hargast and the Shakespeare Collections at the Shakespeare Centre Library and Archive, the Shakespeare Birthplace Trust, Stratford-upon-Avon, Warwickshire, England; Jim Houghton, Nicole Martorana, and the Signature Theatre Company; Agnes Fisher and Simon & Schuster; Ann Schneider and *Vanity Fair*; Carol Greunke and the Max Waldman Archive; Michael Wilson; Marsha Seeman and the Writers Guild of America; and Steven Padla and Yale Repertory Theatre.

Finally, our thanks to the playwrights, those contained in these pages as both contributors and subjects of essays—and all of those not appearing here as well. Collectively, they are the foundation of the theatre, and we thank them for provoking, entertaining, confounding, and inspiring us in our shared love of this ancient but ever-new creative expression—live theatre—whether it's found in a school auditorium or on a Broadway stage.

THE AMERICAN
THEATRE WING

AMERICAN
THEATRE
WING
Founder of the Tony Awards®

Dedicated to promoting excellence and education in theatre, the American Theatre Wing has been intertwined with American theatrical life for the better part of the last century. It focuses today on illuminating the making of theatre through the words of the people who make theatre.

Creating opportunities for students, general audiences, and even those working in the field to expand their knowledge of theatre, the not-for-profit ATW is best known for creating the premier award for artists working on Broadway, the Antoinette Perry "Tony" Awards. Awarded annually since 1947, the Tonys have evolved from a private dinner for those in the industry into a gala celebration of Broadway that is seen across the country and around the world. Presented in partnership with the Broadway League since 1967 and broadcast annually on CBS since 1978, the Tony Awards are at once the highest recognition of achievement on Broadway and a national event that celebrates the vitality of live theatre.

Yet the Tonys are but one of ATW's long-running programs. For nearly fifty years, ATW has made a practice of providing support to New York City not-for-profit theatre companies, as well as to students at select New York theatre schools, through its Grants and Scholarship Program. Each year ATW makes grants which in aggregate make up ten percent of the organization's budget. Over the lifetime of the program, ATW has distributed almost $3 million in support.

The *Working in the Theatre* television program, celebrating its thirtieth anniversary in 2009, has captured more than four hundred hours of oral history on and insight into theatre as the longest-running theatrical discussion series of its kind, offering sustained conversation between theatre artists. It is broadcast in partnership with CUNY TV in New York and various cable outlets nationally, in addition to its online presence.

Complementing these long-running programs, ATW has expanded into several new initiatives which broaden its reach. The year 2004 saw the debut of *Downstage Center*, a weekly theatrical interview show produced in partnership with XM Satellite Radio. These in-depth interviews chronicle not only the current work of theatre artists, but their entire careers, in lively, free-ranging conversations. Two hundred twenty-seven programs were produced through late 2008, and the series returned as Internet-only programming the following year. The complete archive remains a vital resource online.

In 2005 ATW introduced the Theatre Intern Group, a professional and social networking association of interns working in both commercial and not-for-profit theatre offices across New York City. Monthly meetings feature panels of experts exploring the many opportunities available to young people entering the field, even as the meetings serve to build professional connections that will sustain the members as they advance in their careers.

The year 2005 also marked the debut of SpringboardNYC, a two-week boot camp of theatrical immersion designed for college students and recent graduates aspiring to careers as performers. Over the course of the session, activities range from sessions on audition technique and finding an agent to talks with prominent professionals to advice on the financial aspects of working in theatre and living in New York City.

The American Theatre Wing maintains a complete archive of its media work on its Web site, www.americantheatrewing.org, where its programs are available free on demand. This continually growing resource features more than six hundred and fifty hours of audio and video material that can't be found anywhere else, including "Masters of the Stage," archival materials made available for the first time thanks to a new partnership with the Stage Directors and Choreographers Foundation.

In 2008 ATW became the new home of the Jonathan Larson® Grants, which recognize emerging writing talents in the field of musical theatre. Begun by the Larson family to commemorate the gifted composer of *Rent*, the grants are an affirmation to the recipients of their efforts to sustain and expand upon the theatrical legacy embodied by Jonathan Larson's own work.

The current activities of the American Theatre Wing are part of a continuum of the organization's service to the field dating back more than sixty years, when ATW was founded as part of the home front effort to support, first, the British troops, and later, our own soldiers fighting in World War II. ATW captured the public imagination in its early years by creating the Stage Door Canteens, clubs for servicemen staffed by volunteers from the entertainment community, which spawned branches across the United States and in Europe, in addition to a major motion picture and a weekly radio program. When the war ended, ATW turned its attention to the men returning from war by creating the American Theatre Wing Professional Theatre School, which for twenty years was a cornerstone in theatrical training that boasted such graduates as Tony Bennett and James Earl Jones. At the same time, ATW brought theatre into hospitals and mental health care facilities as both entertainment and therapy.

From its wartime roots to its ongoing efforts to support theatre across the country, the American Theatre Wing continues to evolve to serve the needs of all who are committed to the theatre, whether they are students, ticket buyers, or those who create the work we all love.

Also by Ben Hodges

Theatre World annual (Applause)

The Commercial Theater Institute Guide to Producing Plays and Musicals (Applause)

Forbidden Acts: Pioneering Gay and Lesbian Plays of the Twentieth Century (Applause)

Outplays: Landmark Gay and Lesbian Plays of the Twentieth Century (Alyson)

Also from the American Theatre Wing

Acting: Working in the Theatre (Continuum)

Producing and the Theatre Business: Working in the Theatre (Continuum)

Writing: Working in the Theatre (Continuum)

Credits

Permissions for Song Lyrics